THE GOLDEN AGE

SPEEDWAY

THE GOLDEN AGE OF
SPEEDWAY

PHILIP DALLING

FOREWORD BY REG FEARMAN

The
History
Press

By the same author:

Nottingham and Long Eaton Speedway: 1928–1967

First published 2011

The History Press
The Mill, Brimscombe Port
Stroud, Gloucestershire, GL5 2QG
www.thehistorypress.co.uk

British Library Cataloguing in Publication Data.
A catalogue record for this book is available from the British Library.

ISBN 978 0 7524 5831 1

Typesetting and origination by The History Press
Printed in Great Britain

Contents

Foreword

This Philip Dalling post-war speedway book is a must for all speedway fans, young and old. It chronicles the highs and lows of speedway racing throughout Britain during the period 1946 to 1957. You will not have read anything like it elsewhere – it is an historical masterpiece.

It is a book that I have read with great fervour. It reveals the crippling injustices meted out by ministers in HM Government and the diligence by speedway promoters of that era to overcome the extraordinary circumstances set by those in power, which brought the sport to its knees through unfair taxation. You will also learn how speedway racing was a threat to the factory workforce.

Philip tells the story of the rise in popularity of our chosen sport and its near demise owing to circumstances beyond the control of the promoters during that era. He takes us through the years of three divisions, shrinking to just one division in latter years.

The hours of research to obtain the fullest detail do not bear thinking about. You will enjoy the short interviews with Freddie Williams, Ove Fundin, Bob Andrews, Reg Duval, Johnnie Reason, Geoff Bennett, 'Buster' Brown, Cyril Roger, Harry Bastable, Ray Cresp and others, to learn how they looked at speedway racing as their chosen career, in a time when speedway riders were the highest-paid sportsmen in Britain.

I have always enjoyed reading of the invincible Vic Duggan and learning more about our sport, particularly when there were 37 speedway tracks and some 440 speedway riders, many chasing team places. Read of the skullduggery and the game of bluff performed by one club to get into the top league of the time – they failed and closed the doors for ever. Read of the adverse effect that the 1953 Coronation of Queen Elizabeth II had on attendances. And by no means least, we find out about the competition from the introduction of stock car racing in 1954. You will learn of the shattering effect on the sport when Fred Mockford decided to close the doors on speedway racing at New Cross and also about the saviour – for a short time – of West Ham Speedway, when it could no longer keep going. There were Test matches galore and World Finals at Wembley. So much is so adequately covered by Philip, even to the death of Wembley Speedway, at the same time as the death of the Wembley chairman, Sir Arthur Elvin in 1957. Elvin was the man who bought the stadium after the Empire Exhibition and introduced speedway racing behind the famous Twin Towers.

Yes, it is a book with so many facets of the sport never told before. I enjoyed reading it immensely and know that you will too.

Reg Fearman
France, 2011

Preface

Charles Ochiltree, the distinguished promoter and administrator who spent nearly six decades at the heart of British speedway, always ascribed feline qualities to the sport he loved and served so well. Only something like a cat, he believed, could so often be squashed by fate and fortune and yet bounce back to life with undiminished energy and optimism.

Cats are the most inscrutable of creatures but undoubtedly build up a store of wisdom each time they recover from an almost fatal blow. Speedway has also learned many lessons over the years, allowing it to survive when extinction appeared to be the more likely prospect.

The decade after the Second World War was the most spectacular and colourful epoch in the history of speedway in Great Britain. It was an amazing roller-coaster ride which embraced rapid expansion, a brief period of relative stability, and an alarming decline. Thankfully, the later 1950s saw a period of solid retrenchment that allowed the sport to not only rebuild its strength but progress to a new era of prosperity in the 1960s and 1970s.

This book is concerned with the story of the boom and bust of the first ten years or so after the return of peace. It was a time when speedway was much more embedded in the national consciousness than it is today, and also a time when the star riders were probably the best-paid sportsmen of the day.

It has become fashionable for historians to indulge in revisionism, effectively reassessing previous judgements on eras and events. There is an element of historical revision present in these pages. The seasons in the late 1940s, when speedway enjoyed its greatest 'boom', were not always as uniformly golden as they are sometimes depicted. Many authoritative voices within the sport predicted a slump long before it actually appeared.

There was always a certain amount of famine amid the general feasting, with some tracks – usually in the north of England – unable to pay their way at a time when others were counting their attendances in tens of thousands. Sadly, with entertainment tax taking 48 per cent of the cash flowing in through the turnstiles through most of the era, few promoters were in a position to make the sort of investment in stadia and other facilities that might have spelled a healthier future for modern-day speedway.

Despite the undoubted problems the sport experienced in the latter part of the era under review, my research has confirmed a long-held suspicion that the 'bust' element of the period, the so-called dark age of speedway, also needed reassessment.

PREFACE

It was in fact an era which many who were there at the time, both as riders and supporters, recall with great affection, a time when the careers of some of the sport's greatest-ever riders blossomed, and when the surviving speedway centres provided high-class racing for still large and enthusiastic crowds.

Returning to Charles Ochiltree's cat analogy for speedway, I am not entirely sure how many of its lives the sport in Britain has used so far, as it creeps inexorably towards the completion of its first century of existence. I am, however, entirely confident that speedway racing, if not necessarily this particular fan and commentator, will be around to celebrate that great milestone in style in 2028.

Philip Dalling
Exmoor, 2011

Acknowledgements

The greatest pleasure to be gained from researching and writing a book of this kind is the opportunity it affords to meet so many members of the speedway family. I have enjoyed visits to the homes of former riders and listened enthralled to their recollections of speedway days gone by. I am grateful to them for sharing their memories, loaning their photographs and other mementoes, and also in many instances to their families for hospitality received.

In particular thanks go to the following whose names are part of the history of the sport (and, where appropriate, to their families). They have courteously granted interviews in person or via the telephone and email, and patiently answered many queries: Harry Bastable, Geoff Bennett, James and Janet Bond, Barry Briggs, Peter Brough, the late Ivor Brown, R.A. 'Buster' Brown, Howard Cole, Ted Connor, Brian Crutcher, Reg Duval, Ray Cresp, Danny Dunton, Reg Fearman, Ove Fundin, Peter Gay, Robert and Madeline Goldingay (re Lionel Watling), Colin Goody, John and Pat Hart, Eric Hockaday, Ian Hoskins, Ron Johnston, the late Louis Lawson, Hilda Lawson, Ivan Mauger, Leo McAuliffe, Ernest, Norah and Irene Palmer, John Reason, Cyril Roger, Eric 'Bluey' Scott, Col Smith, Terry Stone, Ken Vale, Vic White, Freddie Williams, the late Jack Winstanley, George Winstanley, Peter and June Wrathall.

The task of writing this account of speedway in the immediate post-war period has been made so much simpler by the availability of so many records and statistics, generously made available both to writers and to the public through the medium of the internet. The list of contributors to the *Speedway Researcher* website is impressively long – too long to reproduce here – but thanks to all of them and to the men behind the site, Graham Fraser and Jim Henry. Special thanks to Robert Bamford, John Chaplin, Bryan Horsnell, Alan Jones, Glyn Price, and John Skinner, whose Defunct Speedway Tracks website is a real winner.

The vast majority of the photographs used in this title and in my previous book *Nottingham and Long Eaton Speedway:1928–1967* have come from the collections of individual riders and members of their families. In this respect I am especially indebted to Robert Bamford, Brian Bott, Brian Darby, Reg Fearman, Ian Hoskins, Mike Kemp, John Skinner, John Somerville and Barry Stephenson.

Thanks to Ian Hoskins for permission to quote from his book, the *History of the Speedway Hoskins*. I have consulted a wealth of magazines and periodicals, notably the *Stenners Annuals* from 1946 to 1954 inclusive and *Speedway and Ice News*. I should also like to record my thanks to the staff of the British Newspaper Library at Colindale.

ACKNOWLEDGEMENTS

To anyone whose name does not appear in this list, but has helped with this project, I offer an apology.

A very special word of thanks to Reg Fearman. Reg may not remember having to patiently endure the endless queries of a young reporter in after-match press conferences in the speedway office at Long Eaton in the 1960s, but I still recall his unfailing courtesy and willingness to answer even the difficult questions fully and honestly. More than forty years later I am *still* constantly plaguing Reg with queries, and he is *still* answering them with great forbearance.

Last, but by no means least, my grateful thanks to Brenda Dyer, without whose unfailing support, encouragement and many helpful suggestions, this book would not have been written.

Introduction

Speedway's brief period of glory in the years immediately following the Second World War was indeed a phenomenon. For a fleeting and, for many, an intoxicating spell of five seasons or so, the sport attracted crowds comparable in many cases with football at its highest level, and occupied an accepted position of honour in British sporting life.

Speedway commanded national press coverage. Real-life features and even fictional tales of the cinder tracks could be found in all the sporting and boys' annuals of the time. Leading social commentators acknowledged speedway's importance in post-war society. Richard Hoggart, whose *Uses of Literacy* is the seminal study of the cultural lives of British working people in the first half of the twentieth century, classed speedway riders on a par with footballers and boxers as the 'true working class heroes' of the era.

What lay behind the sport's unprecedented popularity in the late 1940s? The answer lies at least partly in the factors that still define speedway today. Unlike football, which can encourage tribalism of the worst kind, speedway fostered a real sense of community, and brought colour into otherwise drab lives, as it still does today.

Those who flocked to matches in the immediate post-war period, old and young, had been through a great ordeal. Although professional football functioned in a reasonably competitive manner throughout the war, speedway largely disappeared, with the honourable exception of Manchester's Belle Vue which, like London's Windmill Theatre, was able to boast that it had never closed. When speedway returned on a regular basis in 1946, it was embraced with a passion almost unbelievable today. Riders of the era may have forgotten many of the statistical details of their careers but the enthusiasm, the fanaticism even of the supporters of the period, is vivid in their memories.

Always (and still) a family sport, it was estimated that in South London at the peak of speedway's popularity, 5,000 households banked up the kitchen fire, put out the cat, locked their back doors and decamped to be part of the capacity crowds thronging the stands and terraces at the Old Kent Road stadium, whenever the New Cross Rangers rode a home match. North of the Thames, in the East End, a similar fanaticism surrounded West Ham, with regular home attendances of 40,000–50,000.

People in London, who had been through both the Blitz and the onslaught by the flying bombs, and their counterparts in badly hit industrial cities like Manchester, Birmingham and Bristol, lost their inhibitions and forgot rationing and the greyness of austerity Britain during the hours they spent on the terraces at speedway. The relief of at last being able to gather together safely in their tens of thousands, to forget the wartime blackout and experience the glare of the arc lamps that lit up the cinder tracks, and to feel part of a happy, singing and cheering community experiencing something like security for the first time for six years, was undoubtedly part of the powerful engine that drove post-war speedway.

For the older fans, there was a strong sense of continuity, helped by the fact that the majority of riders in the first few seasons were pre-war veterans, men in their thirties and forties who also could hardly believe their good fortune in again being part of a peacetime sport. For the children and teenagers on the terraces, speedway brought the excitement and colour sadly lacking for such a significant part of their young lives.

This book attempts to recapture some of that colour and excitement by telling the story behind the glamour, largely through the eyes of the men whose skill and courage thrilled the spectators.

CHAPTER ONE

1946

It seemed nothing had changed

Fully competitive speedway returned to Britain on 22 April 1946, when one of the sport's oldest names, Wimbledon, launched the post-war National League with a match against newcomers Bradford. A bomb-damaged Plough Lane arena was a poignant reminder of the recent conflict, but Peter Wilson of the *Daily Mail*, one of Fleet Street's top sports columnists, was amazed by the absolute familiarity of it all. Everything, he said, seemed just the same, from the clatter of the machines being warmed up for action and the evocative smell of the racing dope, to that magical moment, peculiar to speedway, when the winner crosses the line in the first heat, the house lights go up and a previously hushed crowd explodes into an ear-splitting riot of applause.

Even the crowd itself, Wilson added, had hardly changed over the wartime gap. Except that mother and father, who had been present in their teens when speedway began in the late 1920s, were now present with their own teenage children. Wilson wrote: 'It was as though the seven-year interruption had left speedway completely untouched.'

What fans queued for hours to see in the 1940s. Photographer George Bott captured the action from a terrace viewpoint at a packed Alexander Sports Stadium in Birmingham, as Brummies Bob Lovell (second from left) and Phil 'Tiger' Hart head the opposition.

Attendances in 1946, when Wembley's league matches alone drew more than a million people, at an average of 50,000 a meeting, meant that a notoriously sceptical Fleet Street could no longer try to pretend speedway didn't count. Six-and-a-half million people clicked through the turnstiles of the twelve tracks, paying more than £1 million for the privilege. The previous best aggregate, in 1938 for sixteen tracks, had been four million.

Peter Wilson's impression of continuity was justified. It was not just the faces in the stands and on the terraces which were familiar. Six years of war had left young men little time for speedway and the 1946 teams were inevitably composed of pre-war veterans.

Transport and other difficulties meant few of the American and Australian stars who dominated British speedway in the late 1930s were able to return for 1946. Most of the top English riders, already in their thirties when war was declared, had spent the intervening years on essential war work, leaving them free to compete at Belle Vue. Most of them lined up for the restart and enjoyed an Indian summer. In 1946 Jack Parker and Eric Langton were both thirty-nine, and Jack's brother Norman and Bill Kitchen were thirty-eight – a stage of life at which many modern-day riders would have already retired. The team and individual photographs of the time show what to modern eyes appear to be rather elderly-looking men.

Many riders had been prematurely aged by the stresses and strains of war. Some, including Harry Edwards of Belle Vue and Howdy Byford of West Ham, had endured the horrors of Japanese PoW camps. A new generation would take time to emerge, although many potential riders were already gaining experience on tracks built by the armed forces in Italy, Germany and the Middle East, while waiting to be demobilised.

Most wartime meetings had been individual contests and the revival of league racing revived one of speedway's perennial issues, the question of team strengths. The Control Board decided to start again from scratch, pooling rider resources, introducing a grading system (which dictated pay rates), and allocating men to the twelve competing clubs. The two six-team divisions were called the National League and the Northern League, but were in fact first and second tiers. A free-for-all to sign up the available riders would have been

Many pre-war favourites were back in action in 1946, usually with different teams. Tommy Allott, originally with Barnsley and later West Ham, was back in Yorkshire, at Sheffield.

unworkable, but the pooling and grading system brought disputes and a prolonged and often bitter power struggle between the authorities and the riders, through their 'trade union', the Speedway Riders' Association (SRA), led by Jack Parker.

Pooling also meant that there was one area in which the sense of continuity was broken. The 1946 teams had a strange look for fans old enough to remember pre-war campaigns. Each of the six National League teams received a grade one man and Bill Kitchen, a one-club man with Belle Vue from 1933, was allocated to Wembley, while Jack Parker, whose 1930s career had seen him ride for clubs in the Midlands and London, was despatched to Manchester.

It was entirely fitting that the historic first post-war league match at Wimbledon should be graced by the presence of Johnnie Hoskins, the New Zealander generally regarded as 'the father of speedway'. Hoskins was the man chosen by Wembley chief Arthur Elvin to manage speedway at the Empire Stadium when the sport was introduced there in 1929. Hoskins later promoted at West Ham, gaining a reputation as a shrewd operator and an unrivalled showman. He served as an RAF instructor between 1939 and 1945 and when the war finished discovered that he had been beaten to the lease of West Ham Stadium by former Hammer and England international Arthur Atkinson, and ex-New Cross rider Stan Greatrex.

With typical Hoskins determination not to be beaten, he discovered a new northern venue, the huge Odsal bowl in Bradford, which later held a crowd of more than 100,000 for a Rugby League Challenge Cup final replay.

Hoskins not only held a prominent place in the sport throughout the period this book describes, but was still promoting at another track he personally discovered, Canterbury, in the late 1970s.

There have been unnecessary and often rather unpleasant attempts to dismiss the role Hoskins played in the formation of speedway in Australia in the 1920s. Many places, including the Republic of Ireland, now lay claim to have staged a form of motorcycle racing akin to speedway in the early years of the century. Although there may be some substance in these claims, for several generations Johnnie Hoskins was indeed 'Mr Speedway' and no-one in 1946 would have disputed his right to be at the centre of the sport's revival.

Wimbledon was promoted by another major personality, Ronnie Greene, who had been active at Bristol pre-war and had held a senior position in the London fire service during the Blitz.

In that first league meeting Wimbledon's grade one star was Norman Parker, who in the 1930s had ridden with brother Jack at Harringay. Bradford's

Former Wimbledon Don Geoff Pymar, whose career was to span thirty years, was back in action, but at New Cross.

Post-war fans saw the last days of spectacular leg-trailers like Percy Brine, who rode initially for Birmingham in 1946 and later moved to Sheffield.

Glasgow White City was the first Scottish track to stage speedway post-war. Left to right are Harold Fairhurst, Junior Bainbridge, Norman Lindsay, Ian Hoskins (promoter), Will Lowther, Bat Byrnes, Joe Crowther, Buck Ryan and Tommy Shearer.

top man was another former Harringay star, Alec Statham. On the night the northern newcomers held the whip hand, winning 45–39. Oliver Hart of Wimbledon became one of the earliest post-war casualties when he broke his right wrist towards the end of the encounter.

The following evening a reported 30,000 people saw another perhaps unexpected away win, this time by New Cross at West Ham. The first really competitive action involving Northern League teams saw a two-legged National Trophy tie between Sheffield and Glasgow, which ended in a rare aggregate 108–108 tie.

Today would probably see a one-heat race-off or a toss of the coin to decide the winner but in 1946 the whole double-header tie was replayed, with Sheffield eventually winning by just 2 points on aggregate. Glasgow, a non-league team in 1939, staged the first Northern League match, losing 40–44 to Newcastle.

Speedway was back with a bang and sport-starved fans were pouring through the gates, from Newcastle to Norwich. Dark clouds, however, were looming, almost before the comeback season had got into its full stride. The twin threats came from disgruntled riders and tax-hungry officialdom. The riders, appearing in front of packed stadia, could hardly fail to notice the box office success, and they claimed a bigger slice of the cake. A pincer movement against the sport became likely as the crowd levels also caught the eye of civil servants and ministers. Whitehall officialdom was already master of the concept of 'if it moves, tax it'.

The need to satisfy rider aspirations and pay the taxman was guaranteed to send managerial heads grey overnight. The grading system and its influence on pay were unpopular and the SRA, threatening a strike, succeeded in getting it scrapped. Compromises were reached which saved a resurgent sport experiencing what could have been a public relations disaster.

Grading was abolished and a pay deal of 35s a start and 40s a point agreed for riders in the top tier. Northern League men agreed a deal based on a sliding scale of crowd figures, which started at £1 a point and £1 a start for attendances up to 12,000 and went as high as 30s a start and the same amount per point if the gate was between 15,001 and 20,000.

A considerable gulf between the stars and the journeymen remained. In one week in May, Wembley rode three league fixtures and Bill Kitchen scored 29 points. His official earnings worked out at about £80 and the rider also had income from second-half scratch races and cash earned for product endorsements. During the same week Northern League Birmingham's Ernie Appleby rode in three meetings for 13 points. His cheque for starting and points money would have been a more modest £25, plus anything earned from crowd bonuses and second-half rides.

The cost of buying and maintaining equipment – almost always the responsibility of the individual rider – had to be deducted in both cases. Another major factor when considering the 1946 earnings of both Kitchen and Appleby – far higher than those of the average worker and even many of the professional classes – was the risk of injury, in a still pre-National Health Service Britain.

The choice of a rider named Appleby to illustrate the financial position of a journeyman speedway rider in a lower league team

Wimbledon's Oliver Hart (pictured right) broke a wrist in the first National League match between the Dons and Bradford. The following season, Hart moved to Bradford while Alec Statham, top scorer for the northern side in that inaugural match, went in the opposite direction, to Wimbledon.

Colin Watson, a 1928 pioneer, was forty-seven years old when he linked up with West Ham in 1946 and showed brilliant form. Sadly, his long career came to an end at Bradford when he suffered a fractured skull in a second half scratch race.

was not made entirely at random. Near the end of the 1946 season Charlie Appleby, a thirty-two-year-old Canadian, no relation to Yorkshireman Ernie, was killed racing at Brough Park, Newcastle. He swerved to avoid a fallen opponent in the third heat of a Northern League match but hit a machine and crashed heavily. Taken to hospital, he died from head injuries. Charlie, ironically, had been a rear gunner in the RAF for five years and had survived many operational sorties over Europe and in Africa and the Far East. He was not the first rider to be killed in 1946. Bradford attracted considerable criticism over the shape of the track at Odsal, which was laid around the perimeter of the Bradford Northern Rugby League Club's pitch. During a Bradford v Belle Vue match, home rider Albert Rosenfeld ran into an opponent's rear wheel, fell heavily and fractured his skull. The thirty-two-year-old, who had at first been thought to be recovering, suffered a relapse and died. In business as a motor dealer, he left a wife and a child.

A week later, when Bradford met West Ham, Colin Watson, the forty-seven-year-old Hammers rider and former England captain, was seriously injured in a second half scratch race after riding brilliantly in the match, in which he scored 12 points.

Watson hit a track lighting standard, but only half fell from his machine, which dragged him head down along the track for 20 yards, causing a fractured skull and a punctured lung. His condition later that night was described as critical and he was on the danger list for some weeks. He eventually made a full recovery but his racing days were over.

Speedway riders accept the risks of the sport, and serious injuries and even deaths are usually put down to uncontrollable circumstances. In the case of the Bradford incidents, the riders believed the shape of the track was at fault and demanded alterations. Johnnie Hoskins ordered the bends on the track to be widened, but it was too late to save Rosenfeld's life and Watson's career.

There was no stopping Wembley in 1946. The Lions pulled in 40,000 spectators for their opening league match, a 50–32 win against great pre-war rivals Belle Vue. At

The World Championship was in abeyance in 1946 but Wembley's Tommy Price, pictured on the inside of Cliff Watson at West Ham, won the substitute British Riders Championship.

Jack Parker (below), now at Belle Vue after a pre-war career in the Midlands and south of England, soon established a grip on the individual match race championship.

the end of the season Wembley had three riders in the top ten National League points scorers – Bill Kitchen, Tommy Price, and the consistent George Wilks. Wembley won all but two of their twenty league matches and finished a spectacular 11 points clear of Belle Vue. Bradford had a good first term despite the track problems, finishing third, with Wimbledon, New Cross and wooden spoonists West Ham below them.

Things were closer in the Northern League with Middlesbrough (draw specialists with four matches ending level, an unusually high number for speedway) finishing 5 points clear of Sheffield and 7 points ahead of Norwich. Birmingham and Newcastle had moderate seasons, with Glasgow propping up the table with just six wins from twenty matches.

Despite the wide variation in team strengths between the National League and Northern League sides, the prestigious National Trophy competition was traditionally run on a knock-out basis, again the case in 1946. Northern Leaguers Sheffield and Birmingham emerged from a preliminary contest to join the Division One teams in the first round proper. Both put up stalwart performances, and Wembley's aggregate victory over the Brummies was by a margin of just 8 points. Wimbledon overcame Bradford and Belle Vue beat Wembley in the semi-finals. The Manchester Aces, frequent winners of the trophy pre-war days, triumphed over the Dons in the final by 3 points.

The man of 1946 was unquestionably Jack Parker. He finished the season with 217 league points, ahead of West Ham's Canadian Eric Chitty and Bill Kitchen.

THE GOLDEN AGE OF SPEEDWAY

There was no World Championship Final (it was not to be staged again until 1949), but the British Riders Championship final attracted 85,000 to Wembley. Lions riders Tommy Price and Bill Kitchen filled the top two slots, with Jack Parker third. Northern League men Frank Hodgson (Middlesbrough), Tommy Allott (Sheffield), Jeff Lloyd (Newcastle) and Bert Spencer of Norwich were the highest scorers in their own qualifying competition and competed in the Wembley final, where Hodgson scored a creditable 8 points.

It was not altogether surprising that Jack Parker, despite his dominance in the league, should fail to win the season's premier individual honour. Jack was not always at his best in an individual meeting and believed other riders combined to block him out on the first bend of crucial heats of big events. One brand of speedway where Parker immediately stamped his authority post-war was the two-man match race championship, raced once a month between the holder and a challenger nominated by the Control Board, and a form of racing where collusion to block one rider was impossible.

Bill Kitchen was nominated as first holder by virtue of his wartime performances at Belle Vue, and he beat Ron Johnson of New Cross in his first defence. The next challenger was Jack Parker and he subsequently defeated Kitchen, Eric Chitty, Ron Johnson and Tommy Price to establish his grip on what was subsequently to become known as 'Parker's Pension', such was the dominance for several seasons of the pipe-smoking, bespectacled veteran.

Parker is acknowledged as one of the all-time speedway greats, but his success over so many years – his career lasted from 1928 until 1954 – undoubtedly occasionally caused resentment. Particularly outstanding or unexpected performances occasionally lead to allegations in speedway that someone has been riding 'a big one' – a bike with an engine exceeding the permitted power capacity. On 25 June 1946, Parker and Kitchen clashed in the match race championship at the neutral venue of West Ham, following the Hammers' 50–46 victory over Wembley, Kitchen's team. Although his side lost, Kitchen scored an immaculate five-ride maximum in the league match. The match race series was to prove a different matter.

The initial match race rivalry of the new era was between Parker and the man he effectively replaced at Belle Vue, Bill Kitchen, who was allocated to Wembley.

Ron Johnson, born in Scotland but a Test rider for his adopted Australia and the idol of the New Cross fans, won the prestigious London Riders Championship in 1946. Pictured in the centre is New Cross promoter Fred Mockford.

An experienced Middlesbrough Bears line-up took the Northern League (Division Two) championship in the first post-war speedway season. Left to right are Wilf Plant, Geoff Godwin, Jack Gordon (on machine), Fred 'Kid' Curtis, Jack Hodgson, Len Tupling, Frank Hodgson and Alec Peel.

Parker won the best-of-three rubber 2–0 and Kitchen immediately asked for his opponent's machine to be measured. The bike was impounded by the meeting steward for examination. Two days later the Control Board announced that the inspection had found the engine to be slightly under the prescribed limit of 500cc. Kitchen was ordered to pay the examination costs.

For the most part speedway is raced in an exemplary atmosphere and riders (and the fans) mingle and socialise. But with big reputations and sizeable prize money at stake, there are occasional reminders, like the Kitchen–Parker incident, that the sport is essentially a very serious business.

The league dominance of Wembley and the individual mastery of Jack Parker without any doubt set the pattern – more often than not a controversial one – for speedway in the immediate post-war years.

THERE IN 1946 – *Reg Fearman*

Star Fleet Street sports writer Peter Wilson marvelled at the fact that thousands of fans who had been in their teens and twenties during speedway's early years not only returned to the terraces in great numbers once peace returned, but also brought along their own teenage children, proving the sport's strong family appeal. Wilson could literally have been writing about the Fearman family from London's East End. Reg Fearman, just thirteen years old at the start of the 1946 season, and his sister, were taken to West Ham's Custom House Stadium by their parents. The family's involvement grew when, in March 1947, they were asked to find a temporary home for two of West Ham's Australian riders, Cliff Watson and his friend Aub Lawson. The 'temporary' lodgings turned out to be for three years, excluding the Aussies' trips home in the English winter.

The magic of West Ham in the 1940s, with the arc lights illuminating a fast quarter of a mile track surfaced with gleaming silver sand, and tens of thousands of East Enders fanatical in their support of the Hammers, was clearly a huge factor in fuelling the young Fearman's ambition to become a rider. The influence of the two Aussies at home removed any doubt at all. As Reg explains:

> With that sort of background, how could I not want to become a rider myself? West Ham was an incredible speedway venue, with crowds of anything up to 80,000 in the late 1940s. To spend time around riders of the calibre of Cliff and Aub and to receive their advice and encouragement was extremely valuable.

Before his fifteenth birthday Reg was practising on an old Douglas machine given to him by Aub Lawson, on a cycle speedway circuit. His parents then bought him one of Cliff Watson's bikes, and his sessions moved to the Rye House training track in Hertfordshire and, on occasions, to the West Ham circuit itself.

> On August 1st 1948 I had my first public meeting at Rye House and scored 11 points – not bad for a beginner. The results of the meeting of course were reported in the press and that put a stop to my career for nearly a year as the Auto Cycle Union (ACU), the governing body for all motorcycle sport in the UK, promptly banned me! The minimum age for racing was the same as for riding a motor cycle on the road – 16.

It was an inauspicious, though certainly headline-making start to a career in speedway in one capacity or another that at the time of writing has spanned the best part of sixty-five years – and counting. During most of those years Reg has continued to make speedway headlines of one kind or another.

A cartoonist at Custom House captured the moment as sixteen-year-old Reg Fearman received his racing documents and contract from injured Hammers star Eric Chitty.

The youngest member of West Ham's Division One team, Reg Fearman.

His speedway career became legal on Tuesday 26 April 1949, when one of Reg's heroes, West Ham captain Eric Chitty, presented the teenager with his racing licence in the centre of the Custom House track. As Reg says:

> There were 40,000 people at the track that evening, which must make my 16th birthday rank as one of the biggest birthday parties ever, anywhere.

Despite his tender years, he made an impact as part of the West Ham Division One team in 1949 and 1950. The fairytale start to Reg's career continued when, in the early part of 1951, and still some way from his eighteenth birthday, he joined an England party which travelled to Australia for an international series.

Led by Jack Parker, still at the height of his powers despite being in his forty-third year, and indeed ranked number two in the world, the touring side also included top-notchers like Eric Williams of Wembley and Eddie Rigg of Bradford, together with the sensational Scottish discovery, Tommy Miller of Motherwell. Reg Fearman recalled:

> For a 17-year-old, wearing England colours and riding on such legendary tracks as the Speedway Royale and the Sports Ground in Sydney, and in Adelaide and Brisbane was an unforgettable experience. Jack Parker was the outstanding rider of the series although England did not have a very successful team.

Later in his career, Reg Fearman in the colours of Leicester Hunters.

When I returned as England team manager in 1973/74 and 1977/78 we brought back the Ashes on both occasions. As much as I love Australia, where I am a regular visitor, believe me revenge was sweet!

Reg enjoyed his best year in West Ham colours in 1951, but part way through the season he was called up for National Service in the Royal Artillery. His army years took him north and to a Division Two team place with Hanley (Stoke). Along the way he met and married Joan, who until her untimely death played a major part in supporting his speedway activities. After a further spell at Leicester, Reg and Joan moved to New Zealand, remaining there until 1956. On his return to the UK he was out of speedway until 1960 when he became a promoter (with a spell as a rider/coach at Stoke) in the new Provincial League. From that day to this Reg has been one of British speedway's most prominent and influential figures.

Gaining his speedway education at West Ham and in Australia, Reg learned all the tricks of showmanship, and the crowds at the many tracks he promoted in later years were assured of quality racing and good entertainment.

I always believed the speedway was first and foremost entertainment. I got that from the two most important influences on my career—Johnnie Hoskins and Aub Lawson. Unless you remember that the crowds want to be entertained in exchange for their money, you are not going to succeed in speedway.

CHAPTER TWO

1947

Duggan's year as speedway defies Whitehall

Speedway's successful return ensured that the winter of 1946/47 would be a hectic period for would-be promoters and riders alike. Despite all the difficulties associated with post-war shortages of building materials, even down to the timber and wire to construct safety fences, there was no shortage of people wanting to promote the sport. The 1947 season saw speedway effectively double in size, with a three-division National League. Division One welcomed the return of Harringay, and Division Two (renamed from the Northern League of 1946) had newcomers in the form of Bristol and Wigan.

The really big advance lay in the creation of Division Three, the sport's first-ever third tier. There were eight tracks, seven of which had previous speedway history of some kind. Cradley Heath, from the heart of the Black Country, was the only complete newcomer.

There was no lack of budding riders for a league intended to be primarily a proving ground for novices. Training schools, notably the one run by former England international Harold 'Tiger' Stevenson, were besieged by hopefuls, with many ex-servicemen, often with experience on the army tracks in Italy, Germany, Egypt and elsewhere, investing their demobilisation gratuities into what they hoped would be successful and profitable careers.

Speedway's new Division Three took league racing to smaller towns. This is the Old Deer Park track at Fazeley, Tamworth, once part of the grounds of the home of Prime Minister Sir Robert Peel. The home side's Charlie Oates and Arthur Payne (soon to become an Australian Test rider) head Southampton's Jimmy Squibb and Bert Croucher.

Tamworth's initial Division Three line-up in 1947. Left to right are Charlie Oates, Ted Gibson, Cyril Page, promoter Arthur Westwood, Steve Langton, Bill Harris and Ted Yates. Kneeling are Jack Baxter and Arthur Payne.

Ironically, speedway's success in 1946 was almost the sport's undoing. The large crowds and major expansion were seized upon by politicians and civil servants who, for reasons understandable in wartime with the country threatened with invasion, had become used to running an all-powerful and interfering bureaucracy. Speedway was an obvious source of revenue through entertainment tax but it also represented, in the eyes of the men from the ministry, a threat to the increased industrial production needed to set Britain back on its economic feet.

Speedway had generally been off the radar as far as officialdom was concerned. Now its unprecedented popularity, particularly in London, meant officialdom had suddenly become very much aware of the sport. For a while its very existence appeared to be in grave doubt. The bombshell dropped in March 1947, on the eve of the new season. An invitation to the Control Board to send representatives to a gathering of officials from every branch of British sport seemed innocuous enough and even, given that it appeared for perhaps the first time to rank speedway on a level with more established sporting activities, a welcome innovation.

Any optimism or good feeling evaporated when, having settled down in a conference room at the Home Office, the Control Board representatives were immediately unsettled and discomforted by the attitude of a senior civil servant, who had clearly failed to ensure that he was adequately briefed. The man concerned demanded, in loud tones, 'what exactly is speedway racing?'

The Home Office session was not so much a conference, with discussions about the role of sport during a difficult time for the nation, but a one-way pronouncement by those in authority about what was expected from sporting bodies, especially unfashionable ones like speedway. The atmosphere and tone of the 'conference' was subsequently described by the speedway representatives as simply an opportunity for the bureaucrats to issue an edict. The unequivocal message was 'cut midweek sport – and speedway in particular – or we'll do it for you.'

The very structure of speedway, with the London-based Division One tracks all running midweek evening meetings, meant the sport had been singled out as the most likely to lure workers away from their duties in the factories. With floodlighting then virtually unknown in other sports, speedway would have been the main victim of a ban on midweek fixtures. Had such a ban been implemented, it would have proved impossible to run viable speedway leagues. There would at best have been another virtual suspension of activity and, at worst, a fatal permanent blow to speedway's status as a professional sport running organised league and cup competitions.

Fortunately for the sport, there was an outcry in the national press, with stories highlighting the part speedway, which attracted a true family audience, played in maintaining national morale. Sympathetic journalists wrote stories which produced statistical evidence to show that visits to London factories by stars such as Bill Kitchen and Norman Parker actually boosted productivity. The tax revenue from speedway – up to £350,000 in 1946 – no doubt also helped to convince Whitehall that closing the sport down was not a good idea. There was, however, to be no reduction in the 48 per cent

Lancashire comedian George Formby, a major star of the era, was a speedway fan and was on hand with his wife to open the Tamworth track and give Australian veteran Steve Langton a push. Also helping out is Tamworth promoter Arthur 'Westy' Westwood.

Division Two (the 1946 Northern League) also welcomed a brand new track in 1947. In contrast to Tamworth's almost rural setting, Wigan, based at Poolstock Stadium, raced amid a typical Lancashire industrial landscape of mills and towering chimneys.

Left: Ministers and senior civil servants saw speedway as a threat to industrial productivity. Future Chancellor of the Exchequer and eventual Labour leader Hugh Gaitskell caused an uproar when he announced in the House of Commons that the sport, for taxation purposes, was to be classed as a trial of speed and not a test of skill.

Above: A major bright spot in the austerity year of 1947 was the return to British speedway of Australian riders – both established stars and young hopefuls. Man of the season was Vic Duggan, pictured (left) combining with team-mate Fred Pawson on their home track at Harringay's Green Lanes stadium.

rate, with the grey men of Whitehall classifying speedway as a trial of speed rather than a test of skill. The classification was defended in the House of Commons by a future Labour leader, Hugh Gaitskell. Gaitskell was Chancellor of the Exchequer for Labour's final year in office and his misinformed view of speedway was hardly likely to lead to a tax rate reduction for the sport.

Away from the corridors of Whitehall, the big news in 1947 was the return to Britain of many of the established Australian riders who had been unable to get back in time for the 1946 campaign, accompanied by a flow of new young Aussie hopefuls. Harringay's return to top-flight racing was possible only because of an influx of Australians. Vic Duggan helped make history in April 1947 when the thirty-two-year-old, his brother Ray, Frank Dolan, and an English rider living Down Under, Cliff Parkinson, who the Green Lanes side tried unsuccessfully to sign, became the first riders to fly to Britain from Australia.

Vic Duggan was undoubtedly the man of 1947, recording an astonishing Division One average of 11.46 in twenty-four matches. He carried the fortunes of a weak Harringay throughout the campaign, with the main support coming from brother Ray, Dolan and fellow Australian Jack Arnfield. Duggan had ridden in England pre-war, for Hackney Wick, Bristol and Wimbledon. In the truncated season of 1939 he qualified for the World Championship Final which in the event was never contested, and also made pre-war Test appearances for Australia against England.

When Australian speedway was revived after the end of hostilities, Duggan established himself as the force to be reckoned with. Before flying to England to join Harringay, he won the 1947 Australian championship. Although he was clearly on form, the scale of Duggan's 1947 British exploits could not have been predicted. In addition to his amazing consistency in Division One matches, he also enjoyed much wider success. He scored 972 points out of a possible 1,044 in all competitions, easily coming out on top in most of his on-track encounters with the leading English duo of Parker and Kitchen. Throughout a classic season, on the London circuits, and in the provinces at Belle Vue and Bradford, fans watched Duggan with a mixture of awe and admiration.

Over a five-week period to the end of May he scored 254 points out of a possible 261, culminating in an unbeaten performance to become London Riders' champion. In June, he won 55 races out of 59 starts as his run continued and the big names of British speedway paid the price. Duggan met Wembley skipper Kitchen on 43 occasions through the season and won 34 of the encounters. When up against Belle Vue's Parker, Duggan won 21 out of 28 races.

He took the coveted match race championship from Parker with two straight wins, which set up a clash with his first nominated challenger, Bill Kitchen. On 1 August at Harringay, Duggan scored 12 points as the Racers lost 39–44 to New Cross in a Division One match, and then lost out to Kitchen in the first leg of the match race. The scene shifted to Wembley on 7 August when Harringay put up a good fight in a National Trophy match against the Lions, losing 61–45, with Duggan contributing 15 points. He then beat Kitchen in the match race clash, levelling the score and setting up a decider.

The prestigious and valuable match race championship was always a controversial competition. Now there were allegations of race-fixing and Duggan and Kitchen were called before a Control Board enquiry at which evidence was given by the official who had been the steward for both the Harringay and Wembley legs.

The Control Board tended to be high-handed. Before the hearing neither rider was given any details of the charges against them. The board subsequently issued a statement saying that it did not consider the riders to have been guilty of conduct prejudicial to the sport, but added that if any case of its kind arose in the future, and the evidence was such as to satisfy an inquiry that there had been 'fixing' of a race, 'most drastic action' would be taken.

After a considerable delay, on 20 September, at the neutral venue of Belle Vue, Duggan beat Kitchen in two straight runs to retain the title. The controversy however had understandably upset the Australian, who clearly resented the Control Board's actions. He immediately resigned the title and stated that he would not compete in the competition again.

The grizzled Duggan enjoyed a phenomenal individual season in 1947, averaging nearly 11½ points in league racing.

The scene was set for Jack Parker to regain the match race crown. The Belle Vue rider also enjoyed a rare triumph over Duggan, in the season's most prominent event, the *Sunday Dispatch*-sponsored Riders Championship. The event, in 1947, was the equivalent of the still-suspended World Championship. In the Riders Championship qualifying competition, Duggan tore up the record books by recording the maximum 60 points from his four meetings, 15 points ahead of his closest challenger. Success at Wembley looked assured. Parker, still at the height of his powers, believed otherwise.

When the two riders clashed in heat eight, Parker, who in crucial clashes often seemed able to summon up an almost superhuman amount of drive or extra speed, beat the Australian phenomenon from behind. Duggan won heat ten but then had a fall and did not take his final scheduled ride. He finished in seventh place, with just 8 points.

The Wembley final supported the belief that no-one, particularly in a sport that relies on good fortune as well as skill, can be absolutely invincible. Vic Duggan, in 1947, nevertheless came pretty close to demolishing that theory.

The epic clashes between Duggan, Parker and Kitchen served to illustrate that in 1947, individual battles between top riders were still a huge attraction to fans. The meetings between the trio, and other leading stars of the day, often caused the 'house full' notices to go up at the tracks, and attracted media coverage that would be unthinkable today.

In 1947 the *Daily Mail* conducted a sports popularity poll in which speedway ranked fourth behind soccer, cricket and boxing and finished well ahead of racing, rugby union, tennis and golf – sports which today rate huge media coverage in newspapers. Speedway riders were almost certainly the highest-paid sportsmen in Britain, at a time when both professional footballers and cricketers earned a relatively low and strictly controlled wage, and rugby, tennis and golf were still largely amateur. Vic Duggan's earnings for the season were estimated by the media as topping £5,000, a huge sum for the times, although in real terms nothing like the amounts earned post-millennium by many sportsmen and women.

Away from the individual battles, the Division One title was won by Wembley, comfortably ahead of Belle Vue. Although the score charts at all of the Division One and Division Two tracks were still dominated by pre-war riders, a new order was starting to

make its mark, with the emergence of English prospects such as Split Waterman at Wembley, and Dent Oliver and Louis Lawson at Belle Vue.

Jack Parker and Bill Kitchen made it a double success for England by finishing winner and runner-up respectively in the 1947 Riders Championship at Wembley.

Although the pre-war veterans still dominated British speedway in 1947, home-grown challengers were emerging. Belle Vue Aces Dent Oliver (left) and Louis Lawson, taking a break in the Hyde Road pits, were both to earn full international honours for England.

Belle Vue had usually been the sole northern team at the top level of speedway in the 1930s. In the post-war period there were Lancashire–Yorkshire local derbies to savour against Bradford.

Apart from Duggan and his fellow Harringay Australians, successful riders from Down Under in 1947 included Aub Lawson and Cliff Watson at West Ham and Aussie veterans such as former World Champion Lionel Van Praag at Wembley, Max Grosskreutz at Bradford and New Cross idol Ron Johnson.

For the first time since 1939, there was an England-Australia Test series, with three rather than five Tests in the rubber, at the new venue of Odsal Stadium, Bradford, and at West Ham and Wembley. England won the first two matches, with Australia triumphant at Wembley. Predictably, Vic Duggan was by a long way the top scorer for Australia in all three matches, followed by Grosskreutz and Van Praag. England's scoring power had a wider distribution, with big contributions from Jack Parker and his brother Norman, Bill Kitchen, Tommy Price and Alec Statham.

Middlesbrough, winners of the Northern League in 1946, continued their domination in 1947, again beating Sheffield for the title. The top five league positions were repeated, with Norwich third, Birmingham fourth, and Newcastle fifth, as they had been in 1946. Glasgow again occupied the bottom spot in 1947. The only difference this time was that newcomers Bristol and Wigan were sandwiched between Newcastle and the wooden spoonists.

As in Division One, familiar names with pre-war experience monopolised the individual score charts, with Frank Hodgson and Wilf Plant from the league champions first and second. The race for the Division Three title, between Eastbourne and Cradley

Les Wotton was one of speedway's 1928 pioneers still making an impact in 1947 as an important part of the Wimbledon Division One side.

Howdy Byford (above, left), a former prisoner of war of the Japanese, and West Ham team-mate Eric Chitty shared a love of singing. Chitty made records in the late 1940s and Byford could usually be persuaded to sing to speedway crowds from the centre of the track.

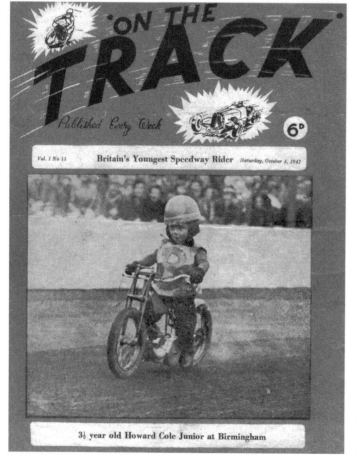

3½ year old Howard Cole Junior at Birmingham

The front cover of this speedway journal cost promoter Les Marshall a £5 fine from Birmingham magistrates. The authorities ruled that Howard Cole junior, three-and-a-half years old and destined for a real speedway career in later years, was being put at danger by being allowed to ride his mini-bike around the Perry Barr track before meetings.

Crowds in the north were often less healthy than elsewhere in the late 1940s but there is a good attendance on the terraces at Owlerton to watch Sheffield ride against Norwich. Left to right are Tommy Allott (Sheffield), Syd Littlewood (Norwich), Len Williams (Sheffield) and Bert Spencer (Norwich).

Heath, was the closest in all three divisions. Both sides finished the league programme on 36 points, with the title going to Eastbourne on race points. Third-placed Southampton were only 1 match point behind Cradley, while Plymouth at the bottom finished a long way behind penultimate club, Wombwell.

Sadly, support at Eastbourne was poor, despite the on-track success, and promoter Charlie Dugard switched the team to a new venue down the coast at Hastings. There were some pre-war veterans in the Division Three ranks, notably Australian Steve Langton, who had a successful season for Tamworth, and Charlie Challis, who had ridden for a variety of clubs through the 1930s.

The scoring charts were topped nevertheless by a post-war discovery who was to go on to a distinguished Division One and international career. Kentish grass-tracker Cyril Roger, on loan from New Cross to Exeter, scored 279 points from twenty-eight league matches, at an average of 9.96.

THERE IN 1947 – *Geoff Bennett*

An overnight success in Division Three was a Birmingham-born former Army racer who helped propel debutants Cradley Heath to second place. Wartime service in the Royal Signals brought Geoff Bennett two significant rewards – a mercurial, if brief, speedway career and a rather more enduring partnership of more than sixty years with Italian wife Victoria.

Victoria, previously destined for a career as an opera singer, was an interpreter for the British Army. Geoff was a motorcycle enthusiast who had picked up his first road machine on an allotment when he was just ten years old. He had nevertheless never ridden a speedway bike until opportunities presented themselves at the tracks in Bari and Naples at the end of the war in Europe. He found some leathers and was an instant success, with a victory over fellow serviceman Split Waterman an early feather in his cap.

Geoff was spotted by Birmingham star Stan Dell, who recommended him to Brummies promoter Les Marshall. After a couple of months at Perry Barr, Geoff was loaned to Cradley, finding his feet very quickly in Division Three. With snow still lying

Geoff Bennett's career in the new Division Three lasted for only one highly successful season, his points-scoring exploits for Cradley earning him a recall to parent track Birmingham.

on the track in April after the harsh winter of 1946/47, the new team's league season did not begin until 12 June, with a 42–40 win at Plymouth.

Bennett made his debut in this match, top scoring with 10 points in a fixture which also introduced Alan 'Whacker' Hunt to league racing. The future England international and world finalist was less effective, failing to score.

Geoff was the fourth highest scorer in the division, notching up 243 league points for an average of just below 10 a match. Such form meant he was recalled to Birmingham for 1948 and after one season in Division Two, found himself at the sport's top level when the Brummies were promoted. He proved a considerable success in Division One but missed the camaraderie of the lower league.

I was perhaps never really completely at home in the speedway world, particularly in Division One. I always considered myself first and foremost a family man, with lots of other interests.

In Division Three I can remember the willingness of other riders to help out an opponent. Most of the men at that level had been in the forces, while in Division One a lot of the riders were pre-war veterans who had not had the same wartime experiences.

On one occasion at Exeter I noticed my exhaust was glowing red, which indicated that I had magneto trouble. I remember it was Cyril Roger who helped get a magneto from an Exeter machine and put it on my bike. I got 6 points against Exeter using that magneto, but it was not the sort of thing anyone bothered about at that time.

In contrast, on one occasion at Birmingham, I was preparing to go out in a second half scratch race against Wilbur Lamoreaux, Jack Parker and Graham Warren. Warren, not always the most modest of men, said to Parker and Wilbur, in my hearing: 'We only need Vic Duggan to have the best four riders in the world in one race.'

That to me was like a red rag to a bull. I made up my mind on the spot that I was going to win that race, and I did!

Geoff's years in Division One with the Brummies gave him the chance to see many of the great names of the period in action. He admired Parker as a clever rider who put considerable psychological pressure on opponents, 'sitting on their tails trying to force them into errors.' Warren, on the other hand, Geoff remembers as a rider with excellent equipment and 'so much power, no wonder he fell off as often as he did.'

Geoff Bennett settled quickly into the top level of speedway, averaging nearly 7 points a match in his first Division One campaign with Birmingham. His all-action style is obvious as he makes a determined attempt to get round the opposition.

This one goes faster, says Geoff Bennett to a cycle speedway rider being allowed to get the feel of Birmingham's Alexander Stadium track. Bennett's own introduction to the sport was on British Army speedways in Italy.

I remember riding against Graham at a practice session at Tamworth, using a new brand of tyre. I beat him to the first turn every time and he didn't like it. He had to win all the time and his all-out style meant he suffered a lot of injuries.

Parker and Kitchen used a lot of guile and gamesmanship rather than just going at it hell for leather like Graham, and they kept on riding at the top of the game until they were old men.

Geoff's own career was effectively ended by a serious leg injury, which put him out of the sport for ten months.

The cause of the accident was unusual. The front wheel of the rider in front of me actually dropped out of the forks and obviously he came down. Although I managed to lay my bike down I couldn't avoid hitting him broadside on and I sustained a compound fracture of the right leg.

Although Geoff's leg eventually healed, much of his enthusiasm for the sport had gone and an attempt to restore his form by returning to Cradley was unsuccessful.

Geoff and Victoria have six talented, highly musical and multilingual children. After Geoff's speedway career ended he owned a motorcycle business, a hotel in the Dolomites, and a restaurant in Menorca, in addition to living in Rome.

His fame as an Army speedway rider, known throughout Italy as 'Signalman Bennett', led to an amusing incident at the end of the war. Geoff and some companions were travelling through Italy by train, when they were joined in their compartment by another soldier who, after a while, revealed that *he* was Signalman Bennett.

As Geoff admits today, they do say that imitation is the sincerest form of flattery.

CHAPTER THREE

1948

Aussies dominate but fail the ultimate tests

The men from Down Under, as ever hungry for points and glory, were again speedway's headline-makers in 1948. Vic Duggan's run of success continued with victory in the Riders Championship final at Wembley, where the presence of the Duke of Edinburgh emphasised speedway's growing status.

Despite Duggan's 1948 record, the season's main stories revolved around two of his fellow countrymen, both of whom enjoyed personal glory while leading their league teams to great success. Only the most dyed-in-the-wool Harringay fan would argue against the premier laurels going to long-serving New Cross star Ron Johnson, forty-one years old in 1948 and riding as well as at any stage in his long career.

The idol of the New Cross fans and a fixture in the Rangers team since the promotion switched from Crystal Palace in 1934, Johnson was one of the real stars of the post-war revival. Born in Scotland in 1907 and taken to Australia as a child, he won an unofficial London Riders Championship in 1945 when New Cross ran a short series of meetings, and triumphed again when the coveted trophy achieved official status once more in 1946.

Vic Duggan, at the peak of his career, lifted the British Riders Championship in 1948 from fellow countryman Ron Johnson (right) and Englishman Alec Statham in third place.

Ron Johnson, pictured on home ground at New Cross. Johnson led the Rangers to the Division One championship title, interrupting Wembley's run of successes.

In 1948 Johnson led the Rangers to their second Division One title (the first had come ten years earlier) and, in scoring 239 league points for a 9.36 average, equalled Duggan for consistency.

The second Aussie to make the news throughout 1948 plied his trade in Division Two, but gave early notice of his ability to challenge the sport's greatest names. Graham Warren, born in Fiji in 1926, took up riding after wartime service as a despatch rider in the Royal Australian Air Force and landed in a rainy England in March 1948, with no equipment and no contract. Warren's arrival is vividly recalled by Reg Fearman.

Graham was known by both Aub Lawson and Cliff Watson, who were living with my family in Plaistow. Graham actually knocked on West Ham's door but Arthur Atkinson and Stan Greatrex turned him down.

I remember Graham well as he lodged for a short time in the house next door. I can see him now with his blonde hair, sky-blue trousers, regulation Aussie three-quarter black leather jacket, collar and tie.

Warren may have been without equipment and may have been sent packing by the West Ham management, but he had one card left to play – a scribbled letter of introduction to Birmingham promoter Les Marshall. Two trial laps proved enough for Marshall to produce a contract, with the initial idea that Warren should ride for his other interest at Cradley Heath.

In his sole appearance for Cradley – a challenge match at Tamworth – Warren scored 11 points and broke the track record. At Perry Barr he put up the fastest time of a second half and there was no longer any question of 1948 being spent anywhere else than in the Birmingham team.

The potential seen by Les Marshall was completely fulfilled. Warren topped the Brummies score chart as the Midlanders defied a poor start to clinch second place in Division Two. He scored 25 maximums, and won Australian Test honours in his first British season. The Test recognition was a great personal triumph for Warren, but for the Australian team overall in 1948 it represented the one sector of British speedway where English speedmen outshone their traditional rivals. The Lions beat the Kangaroos, weaker down the order and with far fewer riders from whom to choose, 4–1 in the Test series.

The first two Tests, at Wimbledon and Belle Vue, resulted in 61–45 and 69–39 victories for England, with Vic Duggan giving second best to both Jack and Norman Parker and,

Graham Warren exploded onto the British scene in 1948.

West Ham finished in third place in Division One in 1948, thanks largely to the efforts of emerging Aussies Aub Lawson (left) and Cliff Watson.

There seemed no end to the conveyor belt of Australian discoveries in the immediate post-war era. Ken Le Breton, originally signed by New Cross, was loaned to Division Two Newcastle after an injury. He is pictured with the Diamonds' 1948 team, in his trademark white leathers. Left to right are Peter Lloyd, Le Breton, Alec Grant, Jack Hunt, Johnnie Hoskins (promoter), Danny Calder, Norman Evans (on machine), Charlie Spinks, Crusty Pye, Wilf Jay and Keith Gurtner.

Despite the notice in the top left-hand corner, this is the Australian side that lost the Second Test 69–39 at Belle Vue and went on to be defeated 4–1 in the series. Left to right are Jack Biggs, Cliff Watson, Ray Duggan, Arthur Simcock (manager), Vic Duggan, Bill Longley, Aub Lawson and Frank Dolan. Max Grosskreutz (captain) is on the machine.

on two occasions at the Manchester track, to the Aces' rising star Dent Oliver, who scored an 18-point maximum.

Hard talking off the track led to a much more spirited Australian performance at New Cross, and a fairly tight 57–51 England win. Warren was introduced to the Australian line-up for the fourth Test at Harringay. Riding as reserve, he won his first ever race at this level and there was a feeling that, had he been used in more heats, Australia might have saved a match they lost by 58 points to 50.

The sole Australian success of the series came in the final Test, at West Ham. Duggan led from the front with a maximum 18 points, well supported by Aub Lawson and Bill Longley, while Warren contributed 9 points, including two heat wins, to the 63–45 Australian success. The overall series result led to bizarre calls from some quarters for the England v Australia Tests to be downgraded to a Division Two affair, despite the fact that the matches were still a major draw card at the turnstiles.

Ron Johnson was third highest scorer for Australia in the series, behind Vic Duggan and Longley, with 39 points from four appearances.

The speedway careers of Johnson and Warren show that they had much more in common than adulation and scoring ability. Both men experienced the very best speedway had to offer but both also knew what it was like to hit the depths, in a sport that can be cruel both physically and psychologically to riders who strike hard times.

The adrenalin rush brought about by his success in 1948 led Johnson to announce his intention to ride at the top level until he was fifty. A warning note should have been sounded in the form of his injury-strewn career.

By 1949 he had lost a toe and the tops of two of his fingers as a result of crashes. In August 1949 came the incident from which he never fully recovered. Following Rangers partner Cyril Roger for a 5–1 heat win at Wimbledon, Johnson, at this stage of the season again topping the New Cross averages, fell, was hit by home rider Cyril Brine's front wheel, and suffered a fractured skull.

He managed a comeback in 1950 but the near 10-point average of 1948 declined to just over 3 points per match in a mere nine appearances. In 1951 his tally was less than 2 points on average in just seven matches, and the long love affair between New Cross and Johnson was over.

He returned home to Perth, his fare paid for by well-wishers. Subsequent victory in the West Australian Solo Championship in the 1954/55 season encouraged him to return to England and a brief and unsuccessful spell at West Ham. He was back again at New Cross at the end of the decade and also tried his luck at Edinburgh.

Fellow riders and fans who had known and revered Johnson in his heyday were deeply saddened by the spectacle of a legend, now fifty-two years old and deluded by an unrealistic belief that he could resurrect his career. In reality, the former Test match star, not surprisingly given his age and injury record, could hardly keep pace with novices in second-half events.

Graham Warren's debut year form in 1948 was repeated a year later when he topped the Birmingham averages in their first year in Division One, and qualified for the first post-war World Final. In 1950 speedway journalists ranked Warren number one in British speedway and he took third place in the World Final, with a fall denying him a possible chance to take part in a run-off for the title.

In January 1951 Warren suffered a triple skull fracture racing in New Zealand. Only partially recovered, he left his hospital bed and flew to the UK via New York, to be met by fiancée Pamela Hoare. The couple were married at St Martin in the Bull Ring, Birmingham, on 17 March, with thousands of Brummies fans packing the area outside the church, dressed in team colours.

Graham made his Brummies comeback at the end of May 1951, scoring 9 points against Wembley. For the rest of Birmingham career, although there were times when he appeared to regain his old dash, he was essentially a useful team man and solid scorer, still good enough to qualify for World Finals in 1952 and 1953.

In 1955, his final season at Birmingham, apart from appearances in challenge matches in 1960, injury struck again when he suffered a punctured lung.

Graham was back in England for 1959 and 1960, averaging just over 4 points a match for Coventry over the two campaigns. When Wolverhampton opened for Provincial League racing in 1961 he was allowed to drop down a division. He was an immediate success, scoring more than 350 points for the Wolves that season, although he was not able to maintain such a scoring level in the three subsequent seasons until he finally called it a day in 1964.

In addition to speedway, there were times when he was obliged to take a succession of jobs to augment his track income. One former Birmingham team-mate who came across him serving petrol in the Midlands asked him why he kept going when he was little more than a pale shadow of his former glory. Warren replied that he had nothing else to fall back upon. His latter years in the sport were, happily, more successful and better rewarded than was the case with Ron Johnson. But for both men, the long decline from supremacy and stardom was a chastening spectacle.

Returning to 1948, the race for the National League Division One title was again a north–south clash. The difference in 1948 was that instead of being a power struggle between Wembley, representing the south, and northern challengers Belle Vue, it was a clash between north and south London.

Right: Australians were making an impact in all divisions in 1948. Hugh Geddes was an integral part of the Exeter team that won the Division Three title.

Far right: It was not just Australians in the news in 1948. Canadian Eric Chitty topped the West Ham score chart with more than 200 Division One points but was more at home on the silver sand surface at Custom House, well illustrated here, than on away circuits.

New Cross held off a late challenge from Harringay as the Racers were transformed from the foot of the table side of 1947, effectively demolishing the claim that the individual brilliance of the Duggans and Frank Dolan was achieved to the detriment of team-riding.

Duggan had plenty of opportunities to give the lie to this claim, particularly when paired with the fast-gating and equally fast-improving Jack Biggs. It was the Green Lanes side's best season to date in league speedway and for much of the campaign it appeared as though the title was theirs.

With Harringay's league programme complete, New Cross had the seemingly impossible task of winning three of their last four matches. Three successive nights in October proved the doubters wrong as the Rangers beat Wembley away in the last heat, West Ham at home and Belle Vue away. As so often is the case in speedway, strong reserves proved crucial for the Rangers.

Wembley, champions of the top tier in 1946 and 1947, were shaken out of their stride by having to ride much of their home programme at Wimbledon, while the Empire Stadium was used for the 1948 Olympic Games. The Lions made up for league disappointment by beating New Cross in the final of the National Trophy.

The major headline of the National Trophy went, predictably, to Birmingham, who sensationally beat Division One West Ham by an aggregate score of 126–90 in the first round of the competition proper, before being eliminated by New Cross at the next stage.

Although Birmingham snatched so many of the Division Two headlines in 1948, mainly because of the exploits of Graham Warren, it was Bristol who actually won the league title, by a 5-point margin. Six members of the Bulldogs side were locals, with their captain, Billy Hole, leading to victory a team including his brothers Jack and Graham, Roger Wise, Eric Salmon and Jack Mountford.

Top scorer for Bristol was one of the team's rare imports, veteran Fred Tuck, who was signed from Division One Bradford and averaged more than 9 points a match in

Pre-war West Ham and Hackney rider Stan Dell captained Birmingham after the resumption of racing and in 1948, the team's last season in Division Two, was second only to the brilliant Graham Warren in the averages. Injury and illness led to his death in 1950, aged just thirty-eight. This shot of Dell's leg-trailing style was taken at Perry Barr by George Bott.

Coventry opened for business in 1948 and despite only enjoying modest success on the track, crowds soared at Brandon. The initial team, sporting the first race jacket design of a flat bee, is as follows: back row, left to right: Charles Ochiltree (track manager), Bernard Tennant, Ralph Horne, Bob Fletcher, George Smith and George Hill (team manager). Front row: Bert Lacey, Lionel Levy, Vic Emms and John Yates.

Split Waterman was one of the most successful of the emerging post-war generation of English riders in 1948.

the league. The Bulldogs were unbeaten on the tricky Knowle Stadium track, which at 290 yards was one of the shortest in speedway, and won seven away league matches.

The majority of people involved in speedway, with the likely exception of Division One London managements who had a poor view of the attractiveness of provincial sides (except for Belle Vue), had long pressed for some system of promotion and relegation to be introduced to maintain spectator interest. Nevertheless, during the winter of 1948/49 many eyebrows were raised at the controversial decision to promote Birmingham rather than Bristol. Les Marshall had made considerable strides in increasing capacity at Perry Barr. Significantly, the Bristol management, faced with the reality of a stadium with only basic facilities and a relatively small capacity, and poorer public transport facilities, did not press the case for promotion.

Runaway home victories, common to the top Division Two sides, seriously affected crowds at Bristol at one stage in 1948. The decline, which for a while saw the average crowd at Knowle dip from 17,000 to 11,000, was fortunately reversed and the Bulldogs turn for promotion was to come.

Middlesbrough, Division Two champions in 1946 and 1947, were not so fortunate. The North Yorkshire club welcomed a record attendance of 15,906 for the first home match of 1948. The team's strength ensured a 51–33 win against Sheffield but yet another fairly simple home victory had a disastrous affect. The crowd for the second meeting, against Glasgow, plummeted to just over 6,000.

The Middlesbrough management, forced to choose between retaining a team with the potential to record a championship hat-trick or lose a top man to try to even up the racing at home meetings, chose the latter course. Wilf Plant was transferred to Fleetwood in May and at least one subsequent Division Two match at Cleveland Park, against Glasgow, produced a thrilling 42–42 draw.

The crowds did not return, and at the end of 1948 Middlesbrough featured in a game of musical chairs of a kind that could only happen in speedway. The team switched to Newcastle, replacing a home side which had itself been transferred to a new Johnnie Hoskins promotion at Glasgow Ashfield.

The closure of Middlesbrough was the first real crack in speedway's seemingly unstoppable rise of the 1940s and illustrated the need for success to be accompanied by close racing. Speedway is perhaps the only sport where too much runaway success can simply drive supporters away.

There was a similar problem of a surfeit of success at Division Three champions Exeter. The 433-yard track around a rugby pitch at the County Ground, with a fearsome solid safety fence allegedly constructed from metal panels originally intended for use in wartime air raid shelters, was throughout its existence known as a home banker.

Crowds dipped in mid-season in 1948, as brothers Bert and Cyril Roger headed a team which in the early period of the campaign racked up runaway victories against Cradley by 65 points to 18, 65–19 against Poole, 69–15 against Wombwell, and 67–16 against Cradley again. The talk was of opposition sides being beaten psychologically before the match began.

Even after Cyril Roger had been recalled to parent track New Cross, the Falcons were still capable of scoring 60 or more points. Devon rivals Plymouth actually won 43–41 at the County Ground, against a weakened home team, but of the other sides only Southampton and Coventry recorded spirited performances.

Wombwell, bottom of the league, became 1948's other casualty, through lack of support. Ironically, given the situation at Middlesbrough and Exeter, there were some close finishes for the South Yorkshire fans, but also too many resounding home defeats for them to stomach. With crowds at Sheffield also sinking considerably below the stated break-even figure of 10,000 on occasions, it was clear that, even close to the height of the post-war boom, speedway's support could be fragile, particularly in the north of England and at venues where the result was usually only too predictable.

Saying it with flowers. Not in Eastern Europe but at New Cross stadium in South London as the Rangers celebrate their Division One championship. Left to right are Jeff Lloyd, Eric French, Ray Moore, Bill Longley, Geoff Pymar and Mick Mitchell.

Cash wise, speedway continued to offer rich rewards to the successful, with Division One heat-leaders likely to earn well in excess of £100 a week. Vic Duggan was reported to have netted £4,000 in twenty weeks of racing in 1948 – nearly twenty times the average wage of about £4 a week for industrial workers and eight times the official earnings of a professional footballer.

THERE IN 1948 – *Reg Duval*

Speedway's post-war boom at first meant very little to Reg Duval. Serving as a paratrooper in HM forces in Palestine meant that he saw rather more of sand than shale for the best part of three years. Reg was kept far too busy by the upheavals surrounding the birth of the new state of Israel to keep abreast of developments in the sport at home.

Demobilisation was slow too, and it was not until his return home in 1948 that Reg was able to recall a promise he had made to himself in 1938, when he had been thrilled by the spectacle of Jack Parker and other star riders during a visit to Harringay.

> I was living in Muswell Hill and my father took me over to Harringay, where I was actually born. I was so thrilled with the racing that I made up my mind to be a speedway rider. Until then I had fancied myself as a racing driver but from that time on it had to be speedway.
>
> When I returned from Palestine, money was a problem, so I got a job in a furniture shop to help pay the bills. I was able to join the *Speedway World* training school and practice both at Rye House and then, on a Wednesday, which was the shop's early closing day, at High Beech.
>
> I was put in touch with Jimmy Baxter of Southern Speedways, who ran Southampton and Plymouth. Baxter said he was planning to open at Stanley Stadium in Liverpool in 1949 and asked if I was interested. To me that was like a girl in the street being offered a Hollywood contract!
>
> What I didn't realise was that Baxter was approaching virtually every novice he came across and when it came to the crunch there was no immediate place for me at Liverpool.

The *Speedway World* training school was a magnet for young hopefuls in 1948 and Reg Duval (right) found his way to training sessions at Rye House and High Beech after returning from service with the Paratroop Regiment in Palestine. Reg enjoys a cup of tea with Jim Dent of *Speedway World* with some interesting examples of transport of the era in the background.

Salvation for Reg came with a chance to ride in Paris and Antwerp for pre-war rider Arthur 'Westy' Westwood. After considerable continental adventures and with plenty of rides under his belt, he returned to England and contacted Jimmy Baxter. The five or six novices Baxter had ranked ahead of Reg had either had their chances or been injured and there was now a place for him at Stanley.

Reg grasped his second chance and quickly established himself in the Chads' team, linking up with South Africans Doug Serrurier and Buddy Fuller, who he had first met on the platform at London Bridge station en route to Paris. The South Africans, unlike Reg, were booked for just a one-off appearance in France and had already established themselves in the Liverpool team. Although he didn't realise it at the time, South Africa was to play a major part in his life, both on and off the track.

Reg was a success at Liverpool, where the Chads rode their home matches on the huge 446-yard Stanley circuit, the longest track in British speedway.

Reg Duval established himself in Liverpool's Division Three team in the late 1940s and was equally at home when the Chads were elevated to Division Two.

I liked everything about Liverpool except the 200-mile journey from my London home and the miserably wet climate, which I think is probably the main reason why speedway never really took off in an otherwise sports-mad city. Most away matches, particularly when we were promoted to Division Two were in the North or Scotland, and I was spending most of my life in my van.

I met my wife to be – a speedway fan – at Liverpool, but I really wanted a move further south and Coventry showed an interest. I signed for Charles Ochiltree for the 1953 season, in which Liverpool was an early closure casualty.

Coventry was very different in every way. Stanley was a pretty bare stadium without many facilities, while Brandon, as well as having an established team, had lots of places to eat around the track. As a stadium it really was streets ahead, even then.

Reg was a high scorer for the Bees but like at Liverpool where he was the only Londoner in the team, he felt something of an outsider at Brandon.

The big thing about Coventry was the tremendous feeling of family. Most of the riders – Johnnie Reason, Peter Brough, Jim Lightfoot and others – lived within a couple of miles of the stadium and had come all the way up from junior status into the Coventry team.

I had actually moved to live in Liverpool after getting married and decided in 1957 that the time was ripe to reopen Stanley for speedway. When the government scrapped entertainment tax in the May of that year I thought I was going to make a fortune.

It went well at first but there was a lot of hostility from other promoters, particularly Ronnie Greene at Wimbledon. I was dependent on booking riders that were owned by other tracks and after a while Greene and others refused to let them ride at Stanley.

These men were frightened of any competition and more or less formed a club which was closed to outsiders. They also felt it was wrong that having paid entertainment tax for many years and managed to survive speedway's decline, someone should come along and cash-in once the tax had been lifted.

Reg moved from Coventry to Oxford following a dispute with the Brandon management over its refusal to let him use one of the track workshops. 'I was the biggest loser in the end in wanting a transfer. I didn't do much at Oxford,' he recalled.

Reg and family first went to live in South Africa in 1959 but returned after the Sharpeville Massacre. He had spells with Poole and Oxford again before his British career ended at Bradford after the 1962 Provincial League season and the family went back to South Africa to live. His last-ever meeting was in South Africa in 1974.

As a full-time speedway rider throughout his career, Reg was always happy to accept bookings in Europe. He is pictured in the lead in front of a large crowd in Amsterdam in the 1950s.

CHAPTER FOUR

1949

Promotion fever as the Brummie fans queue from midday

M id-day on Saturday 9 April 1949. The location is Birmingham's then heavily-industrialised suburb of Perry Barr. Soon the smoke from the tall chimneys will die away and the sound of factory hooters will signal a rush of workers – Saturday mornings are still part of the working week – through the gates.

Not everyone, however, will head for home or the pub. Some peel off from the general throng to join little knots of people gathered around the entrances to the Alexander Sports Stadium, home of the famous Birchfield Harriers Athletic Club.

The people waiting expectantly are not looking forward to seeing sprinters, pole-vaulters and discus throwers, though. Since 1946 the stadium has also been home to the Birmingham speedway team, and it is the exploits of the Brummies that causes the early arrivals to queue for hours – the meeting will not start until 6.30 p.m. – in a bid to secure their favourite spot on the terraces.

Birmingham are about to ride their first Division One match since being promoted to speedway's top flight and inside the stadium promoter Les Marshall and his backroom staff are making final preparations to deal with a crowd which could easily number well over 30,000 people.

Black leathers and a red B on a gold background. Packed terraces at Birmingham watch Aussies Arthur Payne (left), recalled from Tamworth, and Graham Warren, at the height of his powers, establish a comfortable lead.

The track staff are ensuring that the 402-yard race strip, with a newly laid granite chip surface, is in top condition for the Brummies' clash with Wimbledon. Gradually the riders, a mixture of veterans with pre-war experience and promising newcomers, pull through the gates and into the pits, as the tension and sense of expectation mounts around Perry Barr.

This is big city speedway provincial-style, with an enthusiasm and interest capable of matching that of the London 'big five' Division One clubs. Years later 1960s and 1970s Wolverhampton rider James Bond, a Brummies fan in the 1940s, recalled:

> There were many times when we had to miss the last couple of races of the league match, let alone the second half, if we were to stand any chance of getting on a tram to get back home the same evening.

Birmingham's promotion to Division One had been highly controversial as the Brummies, after a slow and injury-hit start to the 1948 season, were only runners-up to champions Bristol.

Assurances that the facilities at the Alexander Stadium would be extended to hold 40,000 people, and the attractiveness of a team spearheaded by post-war speedway's most exciting new discovery, Graham Warren, tipped the balance in favour of England's second city. The sport was now at the very height of its post-war strength and popularity, and Birmingham was anxious to show that it could match the provincial success of Belle Vue and Bradford, and compete on equal terms with the London circuits.

A colourful Brummies team, high attendances and the showmanship of publicity-conscious promoter Marshall typified the sport's continuing confidence as the 1940s

Above left: The American influence at Birmingham in 1949. Wilbur Lamoreaux raced just one season for the Brummies, finishing just behind Graham Warren in the team's individual score-chart.
Above right: Birmingham struggled away from home in the team's initial Division One season. Although the riders look confident enough in the New Cross pits before a league match on 29 April 1949, by the end of the evening the Brummies had lost 56–28. Birmingham had revenge the following evening, beating New Cross 46–38 at Perry Barr. The Brummie riders are, from left to right, Stan Dell, Graham Warren, Arthur Payne, Geoff Bennett and Dick Tolley.

Above left: The World Championship returned in 1949 and saw the second one-nation whitewash in the history of the competition. For the first – and the last – time it was three Englishmen who occupied the podium – left to right: runner-up Jack Parker, champion Tommy Price and third-placed Louis Lawson.
Above right: Normal service was resumed in Division One with Wembley taking the title comfortably ahead of old rivals Belle Vue. Left to right are Freddie Williams, Jack Gates, Alec Jackson (manager), Bruce Abernethy, Den Cosby, Alf Bottoms, Bob Wells, Bill Kitchen (on machine), Bill Gilbert, Tommy Price, Buster Brown and Split Waterman.

drew to a close. Birmingham won their first match in the top flight by 46–35, with Warren dropping his only point to Wimbledon's veteran star Alec Statham.

The Brummies total owed a great deal to Australia, as the second highest scorer was Warren's fellow countryman Arthur Payne. There was good back-up from Birmingham-born Geoff Bennett, recalled to his home club after great success with Cradley Heath in 1947, the inaugural year of Division Three.

Despite this early season success, there were to be plenty of disappointments for the Perry Barr crowd, as the Brummies finished next to the bottom of Division One. Nevertheless, the speedway media considered the racing at Perry Barr to be among the best in the country, and the Birmingham crowd, enthused by seeing the best riders in the world, never lost its enthusiasm.

Elsewhere, 1949 was the season that saw the return of the World Championship. Starting life in 1929 as the Star Championship, the event, renamed for 1936, straightaway gained a reputation for high drama and controversy. Belle Vue's Oliver Langton won the first final at Wembley on the night. Because of a system which allowed bonus points from qualifying rounds to be taken into consideration, Australian Lionel Van Praag of Wembley was declared World Champion. Pictures taken after the presentation show a clearly disgruntled Langton.

The competition continued in 1937 and 1938 with victories for Jack Milne of the USA and Bluey Wilkinson of Australia. The 1939 final was not raced owing to the declaration of war.

Prior to 1949 there had been some individual successes for Englishmen on what amounted to a world stage. Langton and Jack Parker had won the Star Championship, and Parker and Tommy Price, together with Australian Vic Duggan, had recorded victories in the British Riders Championship in the first three post-war seasons. Now the fans were asking whether an Englishman could win a Wembley final actually graced by the World Championship title?

Three British qualifying rounds on lower-league tracks each produced ten riders for the championship round at Division One venues. Ten European riders took part in the earlier rounds, from Holland, Sweden, Norway, and Austria, with the 19-year-old Olle Nygren of Sweden just failing to make the championship round, after falling in a run-off.

The championship round produced the final sixteen, with two reserves, for Wembley. Twelve of the contestants were English, with five Australians and Wilbur Lamoreaux of the USA.

The 1949 World Championship began controversially when English star Tommy Price was not seeded directly into the championship round. He was forced to qualify through a third round meeting at Division Two Newcastle, where he won all of his races to progress.

Cocking a snook at those responsible for the seeding process, Price dominated the championship round and on the night of the final itself recorded the maximum 15 points

Above left: One of post-war speedway's greatest characters was Kiwi Bruce Abernethy. Loaned to Rayleigh when the Essex track opened for challenge matches in 1948, he returned in some style to Wembley in 1949, appearing in thirty-three matches in Division One. **Top right:** Bridging the age gap. Jack Parker deftly splits the Wembley duo of Buster Brown (on the fence) and Den Cosby when the two juniors were included in the Lions' team at Belle Vue. Parker's age matched that of the two Wembley riders put together. **Above right:** Jack Parker was ranked number one in Division One for 1949 and West Ham's Aub Lawson was close behind in fourth spot. There is little to separate the two riders in a league clash at Belle Vue during the season.

from his five rides, to edge out Jack Parker, who for most of the meeting was nursing a swollen ankle following an incident in his first race, and Louis Lawson.

Aged thirty-eight in 1949, Price had started racing speedway in the mid-1930s and was loaned by Wembley Lions to various provincial clubs. He enjoyed some good fortune in his third ride of the World Final. He was in third place behind Wilbur Lamoreaux and Ron Clarke of Bradford when Lamoreaux's machine cut out due to an oiled-up plug. Lamoreaux drifted wide and Clarke, trying to guess which way the American would go, drifted wider, with Price taking advantage of the indecision to snatch the lead.

Given that no Englishman had previously won the title, to take all three places on the winners' podium was a magnificent and never-to-be repeated achievement. The controversy remained even after Price, judged a worthy winner by the media, had been presented with his trophy and a cheque for £500 by the wife of Prime Minister Clement Attlee. A section of the speedway public and media claimed Price's success owed a great deal to the fact that as a Wembley rider he had home track advantage. In addition, eyebrows were raised when Price, never perhaps one of the sport's greatest PR men, failed to attend the after-meeting banquet, preferring to return home and communicate over his short-wave radio with a young disabled fan.

For Jack Parker, beaten only by Price in heat thirteen, it was a case of so near and yet so far. The youngest by far of the successful English trio, Belle Vue's Louis Lawson, had qualified in eleventh place and had been unfancied before the meeting. Yet to his dying day, Lawson believed the crown should have been his. He finished in second place in his first two rides, giving second best to both of his main rivals, despite being well out in front at some stage of each race.

My attention was distracted by the huge crowd, 93,000 that night, packed onto what in those days were mainly very visible open terraces.

I was doing well until I started to take too much notice of the crowd, and in those first two races I dropped points to Price and Parker. Back in the pits after the second time my mechanic had picked up on what was going wrong. He said if I didn't keep my head down and concentrate he would kick my arse all the way back to my Nottingham home, I won my last three heats but, of course, it was too late to win the title.

The British Match Race Championship might have proved a consolation, and would have been within Lawson's grasp. He never got a chance to even compete for the honour, excluded by the fact that Jack Parker, the long-term holder, was also a Belle Vue rider.

Like many other riders of the era, Lawson had mixed feelings about Parker:

On one occasion Jack and I were booked for a best-of-three match race series in the second half at Walthamstow.

There was a cup for the winner and Jack was sure his name was on it. I just said to myself, he's picked the wrong bloke here and I was determined to beat him. Parker won the first heat but I won the second and third. He didn't like it very much because he hated losing.

Above left: West Ham. Back row, left to right: Reg Fearman, Lloyd Goffe, Eric Chitty, Howdy Byford, Arthur Atkinson. Front row: Aub Lawson, Wally Green, Malcolm Craven and Kid Curtis. **Above right:** Post-war speedway's prosperity was less marked in the north than in the Midlands and south of England. The first woman to manage a British speedway track, Miss Alice Hart of Belle Vue, took over Sheffield and changed the name of the team to the Tars, but without great success. Pictured at Owlerton stadium are, back row, left to right, Bert Lacey, Bill Dalton, Ted Flanaghan (team manager), Peter Orpwood, and Jack Winstanley. Front row: Charlie New, Jack Chignell, Jack Gordon, mascot, Len Williams and Guy Allott.

Despite the return of the World Final in 1949 there was still plenty of interest in the England v Australia Test series. The result was a huge and deserved rebuke to the journalists and administrators who in the wake of Australia's heavy defeat in 1948 had called for the Tests to be demoted to Division Two level.

Australia took the rubber 3–2, but the consensus of opinion was that the men from Down Under would have achieved a 5–0 whitewash had it not been for injuries unsettling their line-up. Vic Duggan rode in only the first two Tests, scoring 18-point maximums on each occasion as Australia won 67–41 at Wembley and 55–53 at Birmingham, where the Aussies were without Graham Warren, who had also notched 18 points in the Wembley walkover.

Arthur Payne was Australia's highest scorer at Perry Barr, assisted by Ron Johnson and the consistent Bill Longley. England turned the tables at New Cross, winning 62–46 with Jack Parker dropping just a single point, but Australia took an unassailable 3–1 series lead with another narrow, 55–53 success at Harringay, where Jack Biggs and Warren were the stars.

Bradford was the northern Test venue in 1949, where England ended the series in some style with a 72–36 win, admittedly against an Australian side missing Duggan, Biggs and Johnson. Dent Oliver, with an 18-point maximum and Jack Parker, England's man of the series, were the home heroes.

The England selectors were criticised throughout the series for inconsistencies in picking riders, with form in the previous match not always rewarded by selection for the next.

Wembley, having 'loaned' the title to New Cross in 1948, had a 7-point margin over Belle Vue in Division One, while Bristol won Division Two for the second year running,

Above left: The 1949 season saw the birth of Leicester Hunters at Blackbird Road. On Friday 29 July of that year the Hunters drew 42–42 with Halifax Dukes in a Division Three match. Johnny Carpenter of Leicester holds firm on the white line with team-mate Ernest Palmer wide. The Dukes pair are Jack Dawson and Eric Smith. **Above right:** Lancashire farmer Jack Winstanley, who had ridden in Division Two for Wigan Warriors in 1947 and made occasional appearances for Fleetwood Flyers in 1948, rode for Leicester in 1949.

this time being rewarded with promotion to the top tier. Hanley were champions of Division Three which, with thirteen tracks, was the largest of the three divisions.

The total of thirty-three starters and thirty-three finishers was the sport's highest to date, although Hull, racing on a bleak former airport at Hedon, became a mid-season casualty. The Yorkshire club's fixtures were taken over by Swindon, who had started the campaign racing challenge matches only.

A nagging worry was the fact that the post-war casualties to date, together with clubs whose attendances continued to cause some worry, were all in the north. Problems in the south were more likely to focus on opposition to speedway from local residents, which caused the closure of Hastings at the end of 1949.

THERE IN 1949 – *Buster Brown*

Speedway's new generation of post-war riders followed a variety of routes into the sport. British hopefuls in the mid-1940s – the Australians appeared to come ready-made for stardom – graduated into league speedway from armed forces venues, conventional training schools like Rye House in Hertfordshire, and the booming grass tracks of the era.

One of the most intriguing nurseries was cycle speedway, involving pedal power rather than a 500cc motorcycle. On bomb sites, in recreation grounds or in the more remote corners of stadium car parks, in fact on any piece of suitable ground, the 'skid kids' as they were dubbed by the media, built their own tracks, organised leagues, and even rode international matches against Holland. Given the difficulty and expense of post-

The five towns that make up Stoke-on-Trent enjoyed speedway success in 1949. The Sun Street Stadium was located in Hanley and the team used that name, together with their nickname of the Potters. Left to right on the back row are Brian Pritchett, Stan Bradbury, Ken Adams, Johnny Fitzpatrick, Bill Harris and Gil Blake. On the front row are Ray Harris, Lindsay Mitchell and Les Jenkins.

Glasgow was the UK's second biggest city. Johnnie Hoskins believed it could support two Division Two speedway sides and from 1949 to 1952 he promoted the Ashfield Giants at the Saracen Park home of Ashfield Juniors FC. Benny King of Newcastle leads Giants rider Alec 'Farmer' Grant and team-mate Don Lawson at Ashfield. Grant had been a member of the Newcastle team that had moved to Ashfield for the 1949 season.

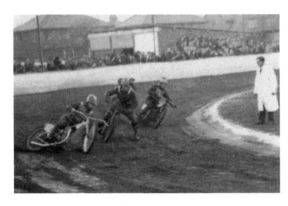

The arguments still rage over this action photograph from Highbury Avenue, Fleetwood, more than sixty years after the shot was taken. Top money is on the rider holding the lead on the outside being Fleetwood's Cyril Cooper in 1949, the year before he was transferred to Coventry, with team-mate Don Potter inside him and the visiting riders unidentified.

war travel, these international matches did not involve actual on-track clashes between British and Dutch teenagers. Instead, they conducted a chess-like postal battle.

The two teams tore around their respective tracks at the same time, on the same day, and as far as possible under similar conditions. They made a careful note of all the riders' individual times in each heat, put the details in a letter and posted it off to their opponents. After the times recorded in both England and Holland had been scrutinised, a winner was declared. Captain of the England cycle speedway team in a 1946 encounter was Raymond 'Buster' Brown, a North London boy who just a couple of years later was catapulted from the obscurity of cycle speedway to the glamour of a contract with Wembley Lions.

Buster was not initially all that keen on the motorcycle version of speedway, and only became really hooked on the sport after a friend persuaded him to visit the Empire Stadium in preference to a local cinema. On Christmas Eve 1948 he found his way to Rye House, run by former Australian Test rider Dicky Case. On a borrowed bike and in leathers that consisted of an old flying suit, Buster needed only four laps to convince Case that he was a natural.

He invited me to stop for lunch and in fact I had my first ever real drink that day at Rye House. I was invited to return about a week later and this time Alec Jackson and the Wembley riders were present. This time I rode a highly-tuned Wembley machine and got some tips from Bill Kitchen.

Alec Jackson offered me a contract, at £28 a week, which was a lot of money for an apprentice draughtsman. Alec also had to pay the firm for which I worked to get them to allow me time off for practice.

Persuading my parents to allow me to sign for Wembley was difficult. My father spent nearly £150 on a brand new Matchless 350 road bike to try to persuade me not to take up the Lions offer. I signed anyway and rode in both the Wembley junior team, scoring 5 points out of 6 on my debut against West Ham Juniors, and in the Division One side.

Above left: Cycle speedway provided a training ground for a great many young men who would later make a name in the motorised version of the game. Future Wembley, Swindon and Oxford rider Raymond 'Buster' Brown is pictured on the far right, captaining the England side in an unusual 'postal' international clash with Holland. **Above right:** Buster Brown was regarded as one of Britain's most promising young riders in the late 1940s and team appearances for Wembley's juniors and for the main team in Division One came in 1949.

It was certainly a dream for me to be meeting, let alone riding against some of the biggest names in the game, and the atmosphere at Wembley at the time, with crowds of 60,000 and more, was something to be experienced, especially for a teenager.

Split Waterman was London Riders Champion at the time but he always had time to spare for me and in fact allowed me to ride a brand new Erskine frame he owned, with the engine that he had used when he won the title.

Tommy Price, who that year became the first Englishman to win the World Championship, was very much a loner. He had his own workshop at a time when Wembley maintained the machines for their contract riders. He was a nice chap but a very private person.

Jack Parker, probably the biggest name in speedway at the time, was asked by a top magazine's photographer to have his picture taken with me. It looks from the picture as though we are having a serious discussion about speedway but in fact all Jack said was 'I would much rather be talking to my girlfriend than you!'

Competition was fierce at Wembley and Buster was loaned to Oxford in 1950, helping the Cheetahs to win the Division Three championship. He then moved on to Swindon for three seasons.

Swindon wanted to sign me permanently but Wembley would not at first agree to release me. Alec Jackson wanted to sign Brian Crutcher, who had made a big impact at Poole and the upshot was that I joined the Pirates as part of the transfer deal.

I did not really settle at Poole and retired to start a driving school. It was not until the early 1960s that I had another go at speedway. The doctor told me I had to lose weight – I managed to go down from 15 to 10 stone – and I started again at Rye House, where Mike

Broadbank of Swindon was running the training school.

John Pilblad, a TV cameraman who had reopened Weymouth, asked me to go there and I won the Wessex Championship. Although I only rode again for one season it was a profitable one. I earned enough money to buy three new cars for my driving school.

Buster Brown had moved on to Swindon by the time he celebrated his twentieth birthday. The admiring looks from the young female supporters give an idea of the glamour that surrounded speedway riders in the immediate post-war period.

CHAPTER FIVE

1950

Speedway pauses to catch its breath

The turn of the decade was the last time for many years to come that British speedway was able to begin a new season in fully confident mood. The number of tracks increased yet again to thirty-four overall. Although Bristol's Knowle Stadium was still under-developed compared to most of the other Division One stadia, a second successive Division Two championship meant that the Bulldogs could not reasonably be denied promotion.

Although promotion continued to be a major issue, with upgrading by no means automatic, four Division Three sides, champions Hanley, runners-up Yarmouth, Halifax and Plymouth – a good geographical spread – moved from the third tier to the second to produce what would now be a thriving fifteen-team division.

The promotions significantly reduced the size of Division Three, which lost Hastings – the victim of anti-noise campaigners – and gained Cornish track St Austell. With ten members it was still a healthy league and an expansionist Control Board granted probationary licences to Long Eaton, Motherwell and Wolverhampton for an initial season of challenge matches, prior to joining a league.

With the World Championship restored and a home Test series against Australia an established part of the fixture list, speedway had every right to feel generally optimistic,

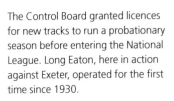

The Control Board granted licences for new tracks to run a probationary season before entering the National League. Long Eaton, here in action against Exeter, operated for the first time since 1930.

Division Three had from the start been designed as a training ground to provide the riders needed for the sport's expansion and, hopefully, to nurture the stars of the future. It certainly succeeded in the case of Trevor Redmond (left) of Aldershot and Eric Boothroyd of Tamworth, both of whom were to become Division One heat leaders and internationals, with Wembley and New Zealand and Birmingham and England respectively.

notwithstanding the failure, despite a massive campaign of political lobbying, to win a reduction in entertainment tax. The sport's general optimism reflected the mood in the country as a whole. The Second World War was becoming increasingly distant, although the Cold War stand-off with the Communist block was about to burst into real conflict in Korea.

Essentially, God was in his heaven, the Lions and Sir Arthur Elvin (knighted for his role in the 1948 Olympics) were at Wembley, Jack Parker was still drawing his match race championship 'pension' and Johnnie Hoskins, after severing his connection with Bradford, was enlivening the Scottish scene with highland flings on the centre green at Glasgow Ashfield.

The first couple of years of the 1950s were essentially the time when speedway was able to catch its breath and enjoy a period of relative stability after the mercurial expansion of the late 1940s, which saw the number of tracks, with the probationary clubs included, treble. Although enthusiasm was still high, and speedway was still expanding, some of the frenzy apparent in the 1940s – the rather cynical and anti-speedway *Daily Express* sports columnist John Macadam termed it 'hysteria' – had disappeared.

Speedway was now in evolutionary rather than revolutionary mood. Changes were sufficient to encourage those impatient for progress in areas such as promotion and relegation, yet subtle enough not to alienate older fans. Most people believed, in principle, in promotion. Division One promoters in London were not so sure about relegation. With the wooden spoon

Wimbledon, rock bottom of Division One in 1949, climbed to third place in 1950 as promoter Ronnie Greene began the team-building that would bring the Dons dominance later in the decade. A key signing at Plough Lane was seventeen-year-old Ronnie Moore, pictured using team-mate Norman Parker's machine as a convenient resting place.

Capturing the feel of post-war speedway at its most intense and atmospheric, with a packed main stand, home straight terrace and pits area at Brough Park, Newcastle. It is difficult to believe that within a couple of years Newcastle had closed its doors.

A massive turnaround for Oxford. Bottom of Division Three in the club's debut season of 1949, in 1950 the Cheetahs won the title, despite early injury problems. Back row, left to right: Pat Clarke, Eric Irons, Ernie Rawlings, Bill Kemp and Harry Saunders. Front row: Frank Boyle, Jimmy Wright, Buster Brown and Bob McFarlane.

going to London clubs in four out of the first five post-war seasons – West Ham (1946), Harringay (1947), Wimbledon (1949) and Harringay again in 1950 – capital city managements had some justification for their doubts.

For the first three post-war seasons the Division One rankings in the *Stenners Annual* consisted exclusively of men with pre-war experience. When the 1950 annual was published the rankings, based on 1949 performances, were divided equally between old and new generations.

During the 1950 campaign, the spoils continued to be shared. The big difference lay within the rankings, where Graham Warren overtook the likes of Parker, Price and Lamoreaux to head the table. Louis Lawson's third place in the 1949 World Final gave the Belle Vue rider a significant step up and the international success enjoyed by his team-mate Dent Oliver and by Australian Jack Biggs of Harringay also won recognition.

The flourishing Division Two began to produce men who brushed aside the supposed gap between the leagues, through outstanding performances in Test matches, the World Championship and other competitions.

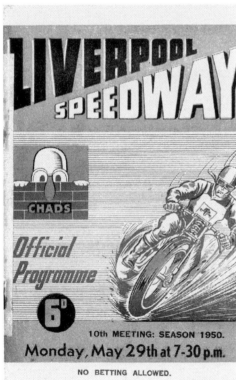

In the post-war era, World Championship qualifiers often attracted the biggest crowd of the season in the lower divisions. This line-up at Division Three Liverpool includes Division One riders like Malcolm Craven of West Ham and Ron How of Harringay.

Liverpool mascot Mr Chad found plenty to look at when he peered over the wall at Stanley Stadium, including the longest track, at 446 yards, in British speedway.

England won the 1950 Tests against Australia by three matches to two, after fairly radical changes to the line-up following a not-too-convincing opening to the rubber. Australia, faced with the familiar problem of a restricted base of riders from which to choose, had little option but to use Division Two men and no fewer than eight from the second tier gained Test recognition during the series. Australia launched the series

Above left: Harringay finished bottom of Division One in 1950. Danny Dunton (centre), tipped at the start of the season as 'a future flyer', qualified for the World Final and was third highest scorer for the Racers. Team-mate Split Waterman, in his first season since moving to Green Lanes from Wembley, experienced injury problems and was a disappointing seventh in the World Final. **Above right:** Graham Warren, pictured attempting to pass Jack Parker on the outside, was at the summit of his career in 1950. He succeeded Vic Duggan as Australian captain, top scored for Birmingham, ranked number one in Division One and was third in the World Final.

England won the Test series 3–2 against Australia in 1950. On home ground at New Cross the Roger brothers Bert and Cyril inspired a 63–45 home victory with 14 points apiece. England's team was, back row, left to right: Tommy Barnett of Wembley (trainer), Cyril Roger, Cyril Brine, Norman Parker, Tommy Price. Front row: Bert Roger, Eric French, Alan Hunt and Louis Lawson.

with a convincing 60–47 victory at West Ham. Tommy Price, a series ever-present and a consistent performer headed the England scorers. Although Jack Parker, Cyril Roger, and Eric French all made contributions, it was not enough to halt an Australian side in which high scores from the established Aub Lawson, Vic Duggan and Bill Longley were supported by 11 points from Division Two's Ken Le Breton and 7 points from reserve Jack Young, also a second-tier rider with Edinburgh.

England levelled the series with a 58–50 win at Belle Vue. Home rider Louis Lawson was top scorer with 14 points but Aces team-mate Jack Parker was subdued. For the third Test, at New Cross, the England selectors made radical changes, dropping Jack Parker as captain in favour of his brother Norman. They also brought in Cyril Brine, like Norman Parker a Wimbledon rider, promoted home rider Bert Roger into the team proper and took a leaf out of the Australian book by dipping down into Division Two and naming Alan Hunt of Cradley Heath as reserve.

England won the New Cross Test 63–45 to take a series lead, the Roger brothers Bert and Cyril scored 14 points apiece and Hunt weighed in with 7. The Australian selectors also made changes, dropping Merv Harding, a great success in the Belle Vue match, and Jack Young, on the grounds that neither had previously ridden the tricky New Cross track.

Hunt was promoted into a full team spot as the scene shifted to Wimbledon for the fourth Test, and finished as the second highest scorer with 12 to Cyril Brine's 13. England's 62–46 victory clinched the series. The final Test at Wembley, won 55–53 by Australia with top performances by Warren and Le Breton, was an anti-climax in terms of the rubber. Brine with 16 points and Tommy Price with 15 were the England top scorers. Jack Parker was recalled for the match but managed only 2 points – the same disappointing score as brother Norman.

When the spotlight turned to the World Championship, there was more success for Division Two. Ken Le Breton had become the first rider from the second tier to qualify for a World Final in 1949, fighting his way through from the first round. In 1950 Jack Young achieved even greater success, finishing as top scorer in the championship round, the last leg before Wembley itself, ahead of Warren, Brine, Jack Parker, and Aub Lawson. At the final itself he recorded a heat win over fellow countrymen Jack Biggs and the admittedly fading Duggan.

Although the pre-war World Championship had failed to produce a British winner, the second post-war final again saw a home success. The emphasis had to be on a Briton as the winner, Freddie Williams of Wembley, was a proud Welshman. Wally Green of West Ham was second, completing a one-two of unfancied contenders. Warren was third, a last lap all-out attempt to beat Williams in heat ten proving fatal.

Hanging on to his second place at that stage of the meeting would have subsequently given the Australian the chance to contest a decider with the Welshman. Settling for

There was no silverware at Custom House in 1950 but plenty of laughs. Malcolm Craven (left) seems to appreciate the unusual headgear of Lloyd 'Cowboy' Goffe, who joined the Hammers in 1950 from Harringay.

Wimbledon promoter Ronnie Greene staged speedway in 1950 at Dublin's premier greyhound venue, Shelbourne Park, using Dons' riders. In 1951 he imported a team of Americans to race as the Shelbourne Tigers. Pictured in the Shelbourne pits in 1950 are, from left to right, Dons Mike Erskine, Cyril Brine, American Ernie Roccio and Jim Gregory. Roccio was killed at West Ham in July 1952.

second best was not Warren's style and in the days of a one-off final, such split second decisions meant the difference between success and failure.

Wembley switched managers, with Duncan King taking over on the retirement of long-serving Alec Jackson, but the relentless pursuit of success that exemplified the Empire Stadium approach did not slacken. Sir Arthur Elvin demanded that his team should not only succeed but should win with style and his insistence on the first rate filtered right through the ranks of Wembley employees. It was reputed that even the rakes used for grading the track were required to stand at attention when not required.

The Lions duly won Division One again in 1950, no doubt to the relief of manager King, who was to be judged by the highest standards. He proved more than up to the task, with one of his crucial team-building decisions proving a key factor.

Wembley appeared to be in trouble in July, when they lost Tommy Price through injury and Bill Gilbert through illness. The indifferent form of both Bill Kitchen and George Wilks also threatened the Lions' hold on the title. King established his managerial credentials by signing Bob Oakley from Southampton. Oakley averaged more than 6 points a match, and provided a solid backbone for the denuded side, along with Freddie and Eric Williams.

When Price and Gilbert returned to action the side was strong enough to cruise to the title with a 10-point margin over Belle Vue. Bristol managed a respectable third from bottom in the club's first season in the top league.

In Division Two, Le Breton, Young and Hunt, already mentioned for their Test match exploits, occupied the top three positions in the rankings. The veterans who had completely dominated the division in the immediate post-war era had disappeared more rapidly than the Parkers and their other top-tier counterparts.

The second tier was producing its own legends, many of whom would go on to be stars in Division One. In the league itself, with previous Division Two high-flyers

Birmingham and Bristol now removed from the action through promotion, a new star was born in the east. Norwich was a successful pre-war centre based in a purpose-built stadium and was among the first tracks to reopen once hostilities had finished. Norwich were to become the next focus for the arguments in favour of automatic promotion to Division One, but the Stars' championship success in 1950 was not enough to secure their elevation to the top flight.

Both Norwich and closest rivals Glasgow White City were unbeatable at home. Disputing the title throughout an exciting season, both teams won four matches on their travels and lost other away fixtures by tantalisingly narrow margins. The factor that produced a 1-point margin in Norwich's favour at the end of the campaign was the side's 42–42 draw at promoted Hanley.

Third-placed Cradley also finished just a point behind Norwich and level with White City. The Heathens won more away matches than their rivals, but lost twice at Dudley Wood, to local rivals Coventry and to Plymouth. Both Norwich and White City were convincingly beaten in the Black Country.

The numerical strength of Division Two allowed a football-style fixture list of one match home and one away against each opponent, and the dates this left free were largely filled with regionalised shield competitions, which proved successful in their own right.

Individually, Phil Clarke and Australian Bob Leverenz, another Division Two rider who made senior Test appearances, headed the Norwich scoring charts. Scots discovery Tommy Miller was the key man at White City, while Hunt and Eric Boothroyd, both later to feature in Division One with Birmingham, steered Cradley to third place. Oxford, bottom of Division Three in 1949, raced to the top of the table in 1950, ahead of Poole and Leicester. Former Hammer Pat Clarke was Oxford's star but he had to give second best in the divisional rankings to Poole's Ken Middleditch.

Clarke had his revenge in the new Division Three Riders Championship final at Walthamstow, watched by more than 23,000 people. He won all his five races, despite in one heat being led for three laps by Aldershot's Basil Harris, finishing ahead of New Zealander Trevor Redmond, also of Aldershot, and Middleditch.

THERE IN 1950 – *Freddie Williams*

Few riders were privileged to have the inside knowledge of Wembley in the 1950s possessed by Lions legend Freddie Williams. Apart from an instinctive feel for the fastest way around the stadium, he had a deep awareness of the pivotal role played within speedway by Wembley chairman and managing director Sir Arthur Elvin.

Born in Port Talbot, South Wales, Freddie Williams was one of the grass-track riders who responded to Wembley's bid to create an all-British team post-war.

Williams, whose younger brothers Eric and Ian also enjoyed distinguished speedway careers, rode only for Wembley during a career that brought him virtually every available honour. As a grass-tracker, he answered Wembley's mid-1940s advertisement calling for young men with aspirations to become successful speedway riders. He recalls:

> When Elvin was asked to reopen Wembley after the war, he insisted that he would only do it if he could have a team composed of British boys. The advertisement asked for motorcyclists with grass-track experience to try out at Rye House.
>
> Wembley encouraged us, trained us and accepted that it took time to produce a rider to succeed in the hard school of the National League Division One. Elvin's vision paid off, not just for his own team but for speedway in general.

Freddie Williams made his Lions debut in 1947 and gained a regular place the following year, in a side unsettled by having to ride home matches at Wimbledon while the Olympic Games were staged at Wembley. In 1950 he was established in a team that had regained the Division One title lost to New Cross in 1948. Few, however, forecast the spectacular success waiting around the corner. He won the world crown at Wembley on 21 September, dropping his only point to Jack Parker.

Although highly respected by fellow riders and appreciated by the fans, Williams was never subject to the phenomenal hype that surrounded many riders in the early 1950s. He was first and foremost a team-man, in a Lions side that won five successive Division One titles. Despite tremendous personal glory – he was runner-up in the World Final in 1952 and secured his second World title in 1953 – his feet were always firmly on the

Above left: Freddie Williams, despite being part of Wembley's multi-championship-winning backbone, was probably often under-rated. Williams is pictured chasing Graham Warren at Perry Barr, Birmingham.
Above right: Wembley in September 1950 with World Champion Freddie Williams, runner-up Wally Green and third placed Graham Warren. The long-term effects of injury meant the much-fancied Warren was never to come so close to the trophy again.

ground. Having experienced the realities of life in industrial South Wales, he never lost a sense of proportion about his speedway stardom.

> Winning the World Final brought me £500 at a time when my Dad was probably getting £4.50p a week slaving his guts out in a steelworks.
>
> Although speedway fans were fanatical at times, no-one really jumped up and down and hugged and kissed you when you won things in those days. When I won the titles, it was just a night's work as far as I was concerned.

Freddie retired midway through the 1956 season, Wembley's last in the National League. After a particularly difficult race at Belle Vue, he returned to the pits and told Alec Jackson that he had reached the end of the road.

> When things are not going well and you are finding racing difficult, that is the time when you are most at danger of hurting yourself. I had a family to consider and I made up my mind there and then that it really was the end of my racing career.

President of the Veteran Dirt Track Riders' Association in 1981, Freddie returned to the Empire Stadium as team manager when the Lions briefly roared again in 1970/71. Whatever regrets he may occasionally have harboured about his early retirement, he has never regretted his loyalty to his only club.

> Wembley was always good to me, loaning bikes when necessary and being very understanding when I was injured grass-tracking. There were many times during my career when I was approached to ride elsewhere but I always said I would stay at Wembley, and I did.

CHAPTER SIX

1951

Tartan triumphs as speedway hits the limit

Nerves began to fray a little in 1951, as attendances again slipped from the high point of the late 1940s. While some commentators in England were predicting doom and gloom, the season proved to be the high-water mark for BRITISH speedway, as the sport reached its peak in Scotland, Wales and Ireland. The sport as a whole reached the limit of its post-war expansion, when no fewer than thirty-seven league tracks set off around Easter in pursuit of points and glory, providing team opportunities during the season for a staggering 440 riders.

For the first time ever, four of those tracks were north of the border. Wales boasted its first league venue since the 1930s, and fans' eyes were smiling in Ireland too.

Not everyone in the speedway world was full of the joys of spring at the start of the 1951 campaign. Although newcomers were still knocking on the Control Board's door, hoping that a licence to promote the sport would be the key to a pot of gold, there were some furrowed brows at headquarters in Pall Mall, London. The speedway authorities and the media were concerned that aggregate attendances had dropped by almost 20 per cent

Scottish speedway hit a peak in 1951 with four tracks and a World Champion. Sadly, tragedy preceded triumph, with the death in Australia in January of Glasgow Ashfield star Ken Le Breton, whose white leathers earned him the title of 'The White Ghost'.

in 1950. The fall-off in interest was not consistent across the country. Some tracks were still clearly prospering, while distress signals were being flown at other centres. A wet summer led to reports of disappointing 1950 attendances at venues such as Southampton, Hanley, Newcastle, Sheffield and Cradley Heath, all members of what had been seen as a particularly strong Division Two.

Despite this, all of the clubs who had completed 1950 lined up for the new season, with the exception of Tamworth. This was no great surprise. The Staffordshire club had struggled in 1949 and were given another season's existence largely through acting as a nursery and training track for Les Marshall's highly successful Division One promotion at Birmingham.

Previewing the season in the introduction to the *Stenners Annual,* Jim Stenner went so far as to say that 1951 was 'crisis year' for the sport in Britain. The big question, he claimed, was whether speedway would survive on its present lines, with a good geographical spread, or be reduced to a handful of tracks as it had after the initial 1928–1930 boom?

Stenner's crystal ball did not reveal the answer to his question – that would become apparent as the next few seasons unfolded. Two of the factors he feared would inflict serious damage on the sport – another wet summer and the continuation at a high rate of entertainment tax – were beyond the control of the speedway authorities.

Stenner did believe that speedway itself could do something positive about three other bugbears – a refusal to consider seriously an automatic promotion/relegation system, the tendency for plans for a new season to be revealed only at the last minute, and the problem of sloppy presentation by some clubs, effectively giving poor value for money. Stenner also had some harsh words to say about 'interference' by the Speedway Riders' Association in what he termed 'managerial affairs'. President Jack Parker and other SRA officials in turn protested their right to have a strong input into issues such as rider safety, pay and conditions.

Edinburgh Monarchs' Australian star Jack Young became the first and only rider from speedway's second tier to win the World Championship, defeating the much-fancied Jack Biggs (left) and Split Waterman at Wembley.

The sorcerer and his apprentice. Johnnie Hoskins (left) cast a spell over post-war Scottish speedway and passed on much of his promotional magic to son Ian. There were few dull moments when the Hoskins were in action on the centre green at Scottish speedways.

On the issue of promotion, the sceptical national media had taken a poor view of the refusal to promote 1950 Division Two champions Norwich. The five London tracks were able to out-vote their counterparts from Manchester, Bradford, Birmingham and Bristol, and their justification for rejecting Norwich was the alleged inability of the provincial teams to provide close racing on their visits to London, resulting in capital fans staying away.

Even more puzzling to outsiders was the decision to relegate Plymouth, who had enjoyed a respectable league placing, back to the third tier. Promoters and riders in Division Two, heavily concentrated in the north, Scotland and the Midlands, did not relish the travelling and the cost of trips to the far south-west.

The move certainly cut out the longest trip of the season for a majority of the second-tier clubs, but gave valuable ammunition to journalists, who for many reasons refused to take the sport entirely seriously.

Scotland, like the nation as a whole, reached its speedway zenith in 1951. After running on an open licence in 1950, Motherwell was accepted into Division Two. Speedway in Scotland dated back to the very early days of the sport in Britain but had enjoyed a fairly patchy existence up to 1939. Early meetings were spread over several venues, including the massive Celtic Park, but after the initial boom the country's tracks failed to establish a consistent presence. When the post-war era began, Glasgow joined the Northern League (later Division Two) and launched a golden era for Scottish speedway. The Tigers were promoted by Johnnie Hoskins and managed by his son Ian, who had served in the RAF in the latter part of the Second World War.

They were joined in 1948 by Edinburgh, racing at a new venue at Old Meadowbank, with Johnnie Hoskins and pre-war Belle Vue star Frank Varey among the promoting team. Hoskins Senior later withdrew from Old Meadowbank and in 1949 opened a brand new Glasgow venue, on the Ashfield junior football team's ground.

The Scottish structure became complete with Motherwell's step-up into league racing. The Hoskins flair, inherited by Ian, soon made sure that the tracks north of the border received more than their fair share of publicity and a Scottish individual championship, Scottish Cup, and Test matches against the 'auld enemy', England, gave the scene north of the border considerable status.

Above left: Glasgow White City's great post-war discovery to rival Jack Young at Edinburgh and the late Ken Le Breton at Glasgow Ashfield was 'Atomic' Tommy Miller. **Above right:** Edinburgh returned to Scottish speedway in 1948 and big crowds were soon being housed on the steep terracing at the Scottish capital city's new venue at Old Meadowbank stadium. Some of the atmosphere at Old Meadowbank – briefly the home of a World Champion at the end of 1951 – is captured in this shot from high above the second bend.

Above left: The Motherwell-based Lanarkshire Eagles became Scotland's fourth Division Two side in 1951. Young Australians were always willing to race north of the border and Eric 'Bluey' Scott soon established himself in the Motherwell side. Scott drifted out of British speedway in the 1950s but returned in the following decade and rode for Glasgow Tigers. **Above right:** The popularity of international clashes between Scotland (including Scottish-based Englishmen) and England rivalled that of the Test series between the Lions and Australia. This is the Scotland team at White City in 1951: back row, left to right: Willie Wilson, Ken McKinlay, Derek Close, Bob Mark, Ian Hoskins (manager) and Don Cuppleditch. Front row: Gordon McGregor, Tommy Miller and Junior Bainbridge.

In 1951 England used a mixture of Division One and Division Two riders, including Jack and Norman Parker, Cyril Brine, World Champion Freddie Williams and Alan Hunt in the international series raced at White City, Ashfield, Edinburgh and on English second-tier tracks at Cradley and Halifax. The big-name England stars could not prevent the tartan army triumphing 3–2. The Scottish team was open to riders based in, as well as born in, the country; Australians Jack Young and Junior Bainbridge of the Edinburgh Monarchs and Glasgow Tigers respectively were the leading scorers, but were closely followed by true local hero Tommy Miller.

The season ended in another triumph for Scotland when Edinburgh's Jack Young became the first and last Division Two rider to lift the World Championship trophy, pushing Split Waterman and his fellow countryman Jack Biggs into the supporting places on the podium.

Even this success proved a mixed blessing for Scotland. Clearly such a talent was not going to remain in Division Two and, with crowds already decreasing, the Edinburgh management had little choice but to cash in and sell Young.

Wales had also experienced a chequered speedway history, with a number of venues in the valleys of the south such as Tredegar, Ammanford and Pontypridd operating in the late 1920s and early 1930s. Cardiff's White City Stadium at Sloper Road was the longest-lived venue, and in 1936 was a member of the Provincial League, until poor attendances forced a June closure.

The venue selected for a post-war revival in Cardiff was the Penarth Road Stadium and after training sessions in 1950, the Cardiff Dragons lined up in Division Three for 1951. The promotion was initially a huge success and because of the size of the first year crowds, Penarth Road was chosen as the venue for the 1951 Division Three Riders Championship final.

The Welsh capital was, however, fated to be one of those many speedway venues where initial enthusiasm could not be retained. In 1952 the Dragons finished runners-up in what had now become the Southern League, but in the following year crowds slumped from the 1952 average of 9,000 to just 3,000.

A Kiwi wearing the Welsh Dragon. New Zealander Kevin Hayden (right), trailing Eric Mason of Long Eaton, was one of the main reasons for Cardiff's success in 1951.

The Australian Test team that won the opening Test match of the 1951 series, by 60–48 at Harringay. Left to right on the back row are Junior Bainbridge, Bob Leverenz, Dick Wise (manager) and Graham Warren. In the front row are Jack Biggs, Cliff Watson, Aub Lawson (captain), Jack Young and Ronnie Moore.

International matches were staged for all of the three divisions in 1951, with Division Three riders having series against Sweden (home and away), New Zealand and the USA. This is the England C Test team that beat Sweden (complete with Olle Nygren) at Exeter, photographed after heat two, which accounts for some of the riders having dirt on their race-jackets. Back row, left to right are Don Hardy (Exeter), Vic Gent (Exeter), Bob Roger (Exeter) and Jack Unstead (Rayleigh). Front row: George Wall (Plymouth), Ken Middleditch (Poole), Bill Dutton (manager), Buster Brown (Swindon) and Terry Small (Poole).

Ireland's problem was finding and training sufficient riders from among its own population. Wimbledon's Ronnie Greene gave the crowds at Dublin's Shelbourne Park a ready-made team to support when he imported a band of American riders in 1951, to race against high quality English opposition, both in the Irish capital and on British tracks.

The up-and-coming Ronnie Moore was one of the Wimbledon riders who gained useful rides and experience at Shelbourne. He finished 1951 as the track record holder and also lifted the Irish Open Championship

Attempts by a consortium of English riders to establish speedway at a second Dublin track, Chapelizod, failed, while in Northern Ireland a promising start at Dunmore Park in Belfast in 1950 failed to progress.

A packed grandstand at Exeter watches the teams emerge for the international, with England C led by manager Bill Dutton.

The speedway decline which was now starting to be visible on the horizon was to decimate the sport in England. It killed the Scottish, Welsh and Irish scenes completely for many years.

Apart from the Scotland v England clashes, 1951 saw a flourishing international racing scene in Britain at all levels. England had high hopes for the series against Australia but ran up against the phenomenon known as Jack Young. Still a Division Two rider, and with only a modest record in his 1950 Test debut season, he steered Australia to victory in the first four Tests of the series with scores of 16, 16, 10 and an unbeaten 18, receiving substantial support from Aub Lawson, Jack Biggs, Arthur Payne and Ronnie Moore.

Britain, as the team was named, lost a series on Division Two tracks to an Overseas side by three matches to two. In Division Three the rot continued, with England C losing 3–2 to New Zealand, inspired by the consistent riding of Aldershot's Trevor Redmond.

The only success for the home nation was a 3–2 series win over the Dublin-based Americans, with one match in the Irish capital and four on Division Three circuits. Scots-born and bred riders raced the New Zealanders at Glasgow White City, with the match ending in a 42–42 draw.

Norwich's second successive Division Two championship, spearheaded by Australian international rider and World Final qualifier Bob Leverenz, earned the East Anglian side promotion to the top tier. Back row, left to right: Fred Pawson, Fred Rogers, Fred Evans (manager), Bob Leverenz and Alex Hunter. Front row: Bill Codling, Phil Clarke, Jack Freeman and Paddy Mills.

Liverpool's Division Two team covered the spectrum of speedway experience, from veteran leg-trailer George Newton, whose career had begun in 1932, to sixteen-year-old Peter Craven, a future World Champion. Left to right are Peter Robinson, Alf Webster, Buck Whitby, Harry Welch (on machine), Len Read, Reg Duval, Peter Craven, Bill Griffiths and George Newton.

In October 1951 Birmingham staged the Stan Dell Trophy meeting, in honour of the Brummies rider who had died the previous year. The winner was home rider Lionel Watling, against a strong field including Alan Hunt, Split Waterman, Norman Parker, Eric Williams and Eddie Rigg. The trophy is seen being presented by injured team-mate Geoff Bennett while Birmingham promoter Les Marshall is in the background.

Amid the year's abundant rainfall – with some commentators taking the opportunity to claim that the newly popular shale surfaces soaked up the wet less well than cinders – Wembley won the Division One title for the third successive year, with a team renowned for its solidity rather than for spectacular team performances – something which seemed to bore many journalists.

In Division Two Norwich eased home by a 10-point margin over the season's surprise packet, newly promoted Leicester, while Poole overcame West Country rivals Exeter for the Division Three title.

Division One and Division Three tracks survived the season unscathed, but the shutters went up midway through the campaign at Sheffield, where the new promotion headed by Miss Alice Hart of Belle Vue was finding life difficult, and also at Jimmy Baxter's Southampton, badly affected by the wet weather.

Fleetwood, Division Two wooden spoonists in 1950, rose two places up the table the following season. Wilf Jay, signed from Newcastle, top-scored. Back row, left to right: Angus McGuire, Russ Pursehouse, Ray Harker, Don Potter and Alf Parker. Front row: Jeff Crawford, Wilf Jay and Norm Hargreaves.

Scottish Cup matches were hotly contested. Peter Dykes of Glasgow Tigers (right) looks for a way past Bruce Semmens of Ashfield Giants.

THERE IN 1951 – *Ernest Palmer*

Ernest Palmer, perhaps better known to older speedway fans as 'Pedlar', a nickname he cordially dislikes to this day, believes he missed the boat in speedway in more than one sense. Born in Sheffield in 1920 and a resident of the 'Steel City' ever since (apart from his war service as a despatch rider and bomb disposal operative in the Royal Engineers in the Second World War – who could ever think speedway dangerous after that sort of activity?), Ernest was taken by his father to the first ever meeting at the Owlerton track in 1929. As he remembers:

> Unfortunately, by the time we got there the gates were closed on a capacity crowd watching legendary names like Clem Beckett, who later went off to fight in the Spanish Civil War. We were stranded outside and I had to wait a while longer for my first look at speedway.

When Ernest returned home after war service, he found that not only had Sheffield been in the forefront of the post-war revival in 1946, but there was also a Division Three team operating at the South Yorkshire Sports Stadium in the mining town of Wombwell. It was on the Wombwell track that he had his first competitive rides, and made his debut for the Colliers in 1948, riding alongside such gritty Northern competitors as Harwood Pike. When Wombwell closed down, Ernest moved with Pike to Leicester, enjoyed the revival season at Blackbird Road and cemented what was to be a life-long friendship with fellow Hunter Jack Winstanley.

In 1950 he was transferred to Long Eaton, a track which had seen sporadic racing in the pioneer era and was now running on an open licence prior to being accepted into the National League Division Three. Ernest and Long Eaton took to each other immediately. He enjoyed his best-ever season points-wise and became a huge favourite with the home supporters, with some heavy scoring, determined riding and a friendly personality which made him much in demand at supporters' events. He retained the captaincy for the Archers' first league season in 1951 but found the strain of leading a largely unsuccessful side badly hit by injuries affected his own performances. Although he was retained by the Station Road management for 1952, he rode in just one match before retiring from riding to accept an invitation from Frank Varey to be team manager of a revived Sheffield side.

Ernest was one of the few riders to race wearing spectacles. He tried contact lenses, but found that grit from the track surface got under the lenses and caused discomfort. Several pairs of glasses were smashed during his career, most spectacularly when the metal shield protecting the engine from flying cinders or shale worked loose during a race, slipped and locked the front wheel, sending Ernest headlong on to the track.

Ernest 'Pedlar' Palmer moved from Leicester to Long Eaton during the track's open licence season in 1950 and was appointed captain. Ernest enjoyed enormous popularity at Station Road and led the Archers in their first league campaign in 1951. Here he shows his determination as he drives under Bob Jones of Swindon, with team-mate Bob Ibbotson in the background.

No casual attire in 1951 for speedway supporters' functions as ball gowns and smart suits were the order of the day. Ernest Palmer (right) receives the Long Eaton rider of the year award from Miss Long Eaton Speedway.

When they picked me up my face was covered in blood and people feared the worst. In fact it all came from a cut just my eye which the doctor was able to stitch. But inevitably it cost me a new pair of specs!

Ernest enjoyed several seasons managing Sheffield under the Varey promotion, while at the same time running a haulage business. He enjoyed his contact with the riders who came under his wing, particularly 1960s star Clive Featherby, while among the sport's top names he had great respect for World Champions Ove Fundin and Peter Craven.

He remained a regular at Owlerton for many years after severing his official connections with the Tigers and is a great fan of modern-day riders, believing the standard of racing is much higher than in his own day.

We really just pottered along compared to the modern speedway rider. The modern lay-down bikes are a lot easier to ride than our machines and this is reflected in the fact that the riders have the confidence to get so close to each other at such high speeds.

Ernest is also a great fan of the modern-day trend for riders to start racing at a much younger age than was permissible in the 1950s, encouraged by training schemes, mini-tracks, and championships for various age groups.

There is a lot of help for promising young riders today. When I started a novice was lucky to get one ride a week and you really had to break through on your own.

Ernest Palmer enjoyed his riding career and his days as team manager and now, when he cannot actually get to a live meeting, watches league racing and the Grand Prix series on television. His one regret in his speedway life is that the war meant he missed so many years that could have been spent building a career.

I missed out on that first meeting at Sheffield and although as a rider I had a lot of good times and made a lot of friends, I feel my career never really got off the ground. Perhaps that's why I get so much pleasure from seeing today's youngsters doing well and being encouraged.

Following his riding career Ernest Palmer (kneeling by machine) became a much-respected team manager at Sheffield and a mentor to Tigers' riders such as Clive Featherby (left).

CHAPTER SEVEN

1952

Close season chess moves bring speedway winners and losers

Rumour and counter-rumour has always been an integral part of speedway. In the winter months in particular, intense speculation about the future of both tracks and individual riders conveniently fills column inches and undoubtedly helps keep spectator interest alive. The rumour mill was particularly lively in the late autumn of 1951 and the early weeks of 1952. Some of the biggest names in the sport were on the verge of important changes and there was a curious, almost chessboard feel to the way that the fates of venues and performers were dependent on a series of complicated and closely inter-related moves.

There was a widespread feeling that several venues up and down the country had experienced what was generally described as 'a thin time' in 1951 and it was no surprise when Fleetwood, Halifax and Newcastle followed the mid-season example of Sheffield and made early exits from Division Two.

Britain's rapidly increasing prosperity in the early 1950s, although widespread, was not universal. Some areas, in the north of England especially, were experiencing trading difficulties and job shortages, and the latest batch of withdrawals brought the number of post-war speedway closures north of the River Trent to seven. The closure notices issued by the northern tracks were nevertheless overshadowed by suggestions that all was not well at the heart of the speedway world in London, particularly in the eastern portion of the capital city.

It was barely mid-October in 1951, with some tracks still open for business, when a statement from West Ham Stadium made headline news. The statement announced that the company holding the racing rights at Custom House, Speedway Stadiums (1946) Ltd, directed by former Hammers rider Arthur Atkinson, his wife Tippy, and ex-New Cross man Stan Greatrex – the directing trio who had beaten Johnnie Hoskins to the Custom House lease in 1946 – had decided not to take up its option for the 1952 season.

The legendary 40,000–50,000 regular fans who thronged Custom House in the late 1940s had begun to seriously diminish in numbers and for a while it looked as though the East End track could become the first post-war casualty among the London big five.

One of the main participants in the bout of psychological warfare that was to dominate the next few months seemingly forgot the subtle approach which characterises the best chess players and gamblers. With West Ham's supporters still reeling from the news that their track was in trouble, the management of East End neighbours and Division Two members Walthamstow acted with what seemed like indecent haste in suggesting that they provided a ready-made answer to the potential loss of one of the sport's giants.

Walthamstow, said the track's directors, was a ready-made alternative to West Ham, virtually on the doorstep. The Wolves management's bid for promotion, which to be fair would probably have been made whatever the state of play regarding West Ham, was based on the sort of logic that is almost unique to speedway.

The bid was based not on overwhelming Division Two success, which was the argument in favour of the promotion of Norwich after two successive second-tier championship titles, but on the premise that a step up to the top tier was the only way to save a struggling promotion.

Despite having the advantages of a well-appointed stadium and a fairly attractive team, the experiment of running second tier speedway in London had proved to be a failure, with average attendances at Walthamstow of little more than 5,000.

The Wolves management believed this situation would change if the team was promoted to Division One. Locals, with the biggest names in speedway racing nearby, had failed to support the promotion, and opposing teams, particularly those from the north, had brought little visiting support. Division One fare, with regular visits from the likes of Wembley and Harringay would, so the Walthamstow board believed, transform the fortunes of the track.

With the Walthamstow pawn set to capture the once seemingly unassailable castle that was West Ham, the speedway world waited for the next moves in the game. The Walthamstow management, carrying on the chess analogy, seemed to weaken their case by making their intentions all too obvious. The track's board believed its interests would be best served by ratcheting up the pressure on the Control Board and other interested parties – a ploy which in speedway is just as likely to antagonise and fail as it is to succeed.

The Walthamstow policy, in the words of Reg Fearman, was based on 'skullduggery and a game of bluff'. It was doomed to fail. Promoter Charles Chandler announced bluntly that for 1952 the choice for Walthamstow was Division One or closure. At the same time he won few friends among the Custom House faithful by assuming that the Hammers were already dead in the water, making a provocative transfer offer for several West Ham riders.

The ultimately decisive move in speedway's most compelling close-season power struggle came from an unexpected source, with millionaire Alan Sanderson, the power behind the Coventry and Leicester promotions, challenging the West Ham Stadium authorities to offer him a deal which would prove sufficiently attractive to allow him to take over and save speedway at Custom House.

The falling attendances at West Ham and a team that had become noted for inconsistency suggested that Alan Sanderson would need to produce something special from up his capacious sleeve if he was to make a go of promoting the Hammers. That

West Ham won the race to sign new World Champion Jack Young from Edinburgh. Young is pictured in Hammers colours leading Jeff Lloyd at Harringay.

Birmingham were the shock team of Division One. Ron Mountford, on the inside, and Ivor 'Digger' Davies try to hold off Lawson of Belle Vue.

Alan Hunt (left) spearheaded Birmingham's 1952 challenge. Team-mate Geoff Bennett's comeback for the Brummies after serious injury was unsuccessful and he returned to Cradley.

is precisely where the other great headline story of the early months of 1952 came into play. Ever since Edinburgh's Jack Young had lifted the 1951 World Championship trophy at Wembley in September, the consensus of opinion had been that a rider of his ability was unlikely to linger for long in Division Two.

The speedway press was overflowing with speculation about Young's likely destination. Some said Harringay, others Belle Vue, while it was suggested that the Australian would make a perfect spearhead for Division Two champions Norwich, about to be promoted to the top tier, a splendid replacement for the injury-hit Graham Warren at Birmingham, and the perfect leader for a promoted Walthamstow.

Just when Belle Vue appeared to have won the race, with authoritative commentators claiming that a transfer to Hyde Road was a done deal, at an unprecedented fee of little short of £4,000, everything came good for the West Ham fans.

Alan Sanderson was granted a licence to promote at West Ham, Young was signed for the Hammers for a reported £3,750, proving to be the perfect successor to the departing Aub Lawson, while speedway's most colourful personality, Johnnie Hoskins, was appointed manager at Custom House. Sanderson, like every good chess player, had carefully pondered his moves, kept his intentions, particularly in respect of his interest in Young, quiet until the last possible moment, and had then moved in for the kill.

Not only the West Ham fans but speedway as a whole appeared to be the winner, with the sport rejuvenated at one of its most iconic venues. To make the story perfect for the media, there was also the irony that the departing promoters, the Atkinsons and Greatrex, had beaten pre-war Custom House chief Hoskins to the punch when the sport revived after the war.

Sadly, like in most tales, there were losers too. In this case, the Walthamstow fans, as the track's management refused the Control Board options of staying put in Division Two or stepping down to the third tier, renamed the Southern League for 1952, and carried through the closure threat. Walthamstow stadium was never again to stage speedway and has now fallen prey to redevelopment.

Despite the various withdrawals, speedway moved into its seventh post-war season in apparently good shape. The number of starters was down to thirty-three from the 1951 high of thirty-seven, but the good news was that Southampton had bounced back from closure midway through 1951 to line up in the Southern League.

The renamed competition also had a genuine newcomer in the form of Ipswich, welcomed into league racing after a probationary open licence baptism the previous year.

Some commentators nevertheless insisted that the sport was living on borrowed time. With no let-up in the level of entertainment tax, despite a change of government, there were claims that many tracks, including some in Division One, were on a financial knife-edge. Alan Sanderson's willingness to take on the task not only of running West Ham but to gamble on the success of the venture by splashing out an unprecedented transfer fee for Jack Young, was seen by some as a huge gamble. It was estimated by one experienced journalist, who claimed to have seen the gate receipts for Division One for 1951, that the fee paid for Young would have effectively wiped out the average track's financial surplus – in those cases where there was an actual surplus and not a deficit.

Australia won the series against England 4–1, losing only in the final match at Harringay with this side. Standing, left to right, are Cliff Watson, Ronnie Moore, Arthur Simcock (manager), Jack Young, Merv Harding and Graham Warren. Kneeling are (left) Arthur Payne, Jack Biggs (on machine) and (right) Ken Walsh.

England's sole success in the Tests came when the Lions were already four matches down. Left to right are Freddie Williams, Tommy Miller, Alan Hunt, Jeff Lloyd (on machine), Dick Bradley (top scorer with 16 points), Derek Close and Ron How. Kneeling is Brian Crutcher of Poole, making his Test debut.

For the Belle Vue Test, England included as reserves northern riders Arthur Forrest (left) of Bradford and local favourite Louis Lawson.

It is interesting to note that in later years it would become something of a speedway cliché to suggest that promoters in the boom years amassed huge profits and yet failed to invest for the future. This may have been true to a greater or lesser extent in the late 1940s. By the early 1950s, it is likely many promotions were taking a loss, in the hope that the good years and the crowds would return, or at least that entertainment tax would be reduced.

There was no immediate dividend for Sanderson in terms of silverware. The Hammers finished fourth in a Division One yet again dominated by Wembley. It was the same position West Ham had occupied in 1951 and in fact, for all the fanaticism of the support, the Hammers could point to just one National League title, in 1937.

Individually, Jack Young more than paid back the cost of the fee. Some voices in speedway, while accepting that the Australian had deserved his world title, queried whether or not he was ready to excel in the day-to-day grind of Division One racing. A total of 377 league points from thirty-five matches, at an average of more than 10.5 points a match, was a magnificent response to the doubters.

Young's maturity and what Tom Stenner of the *Daily Mail/Sunday Dispatch* described as his 'sustained brilliance and calculated endeavour' were obvious in the manner in which he successfully defended his World title. After a fairly routine victory in his first ride over Birmingham's 18-year-old Swedish prospect Dan Forsberg (the first European rider in the final since 1937), South African Henry Long and a Graham Warren who was a shadow of his pre-injury self, Young showed the aggressive and risk-taking side of his technique in heat six.

Fred Williams made the gate and held Young off for three laps, forcing the reigning champion to dive through what was described as 'a narrowing gap on the outside' as the pair headed into the final lap. Young scraped his handlebar and footrest along the fence but clung on and achieved the right angle and amount of drive in the corner to overtake on the inside.

Unbeaten when he came out for his final race, he was headed from the gate by Wembley's Bob Oakley. The more cautious side of Young came to the fore, and he settled for the 2 points that he knew would bring him victory. The pressure was still intense and he later commented that the 70 seconds of the heat had 'seemed like 70 years'.

Young's dominance was also there for all to see in the Test match arena. For the second successive season Australia thrashed England 4–1 and Young registered 75 points from his five Tests. England's much greater choice of eligible riders proved to be of no benefit, and the home side's selectors added to the instability of the team by sticking to the no-doubt financially justified policy of boosting attendances at Tests by picking home riders.

Five Australians – Young, Ronnie Moore (who outscored the World Champion with 80 points from the series), Warren (who returned to some kind of form towards the end of the series), Jack Biggs and Arthur Payne – appeared in all the Tests. England used eighteen riders, with only Fred Williams and Alan Hunt being ever-present. The Lions won just the final match, at Harringay by a 2-point margin, with Dick Bradley of Bristol

Scotland–England clashes, particularly on the tracks north of the border, attracted as much enthusiasm as the England–Australia Tests.

A legend made his British debut in 1952. Barry Briggs followed his hero Ronnie Moore from Christchurch, New Zealand, to Plough Lane, Wimbledon.

Above left: Flying the flag for Welsh speedway, Cardiff Dragons enjoyed their best season on the track in 1952, as runners-up to Rayleigh in the Southern League. **Above right:** Two Southern League aces clashed at Bannister Court, Southampton. Southampton's New Zealander Brian McKeown (inside) and Exeter's Goog Hoskin were top scorers in the league for their respective teams.

Long Eaton folded midway through the season despite an average crowd of around 4,000. Here Jack Winstanley (on the white line) and Roy Browning hold the advantage for the Archers.

Plymouth's Devils were relegated when the predominantly northern and Scottish Division Two promoters declared the journey to the far south-west to be hellish for their riders.

taking advantage of his reserve position – he had five outings in the last nine heats – to top score with 16 points.

Young's promotion to Division One had paid handsome dividends but the same could not be said for Norwich, who finished as wooden spoonists. Some encouragement for the future for the East Anglian side was provided by Birmingham, who had also struggled in their initial Division One campaign but in 1952 were worthy runners-up to Wembley.

Poole followed up their 1951 Division Three title by romping to the Division Two championship, finishing 8 points ahead of runners-up Coventry. Rayleigh had a 10-point lead at the top of the Southern League over Cardiff.

Harringay won the National Trophy for the first time, with the highlight of the competition proving to be Poole's run to the second round of the competition proper, beating Division One Norwich and losing by just 6 points on aggregate to New Cross.

All the 1952 starters reached the finishing line, with the exception of Long Eaton. Given the sad record of sides from the north of England, it was perhaps no great surprise to record the struggles of a small town team located inconveniently between the major population centres of Nottingham and Derby, just above the traditional north-south dividing line of the River Trent. In a move that was to be seen again in speedway as times grew harder, Long Eaton's loyal fans tried gamely to raise the finance to keep the track alive. Unlike other small town venues like Wombwell and Fleetwood, Long Eaton was to rise again, although the average attendance of around 4,000 which proved inadequate in the face of 1952 costs was rarely to be equalled ever again.

THERE IN 1952 – *Johnnie Reason*

Speedway riders naturally have their share of regrets. Some feel lack of cash or other circumstances delayed their careers until they were really too old to make a mark, while others feel in retrospect that they retired too early. Johnnie Reason, a Coventry legend in the post-war years, rues the day he was spotted eating a certain delicacy at a Midlands beauty spot. He explains:

> With other riders and supporters I was at Trentham Gardens near Stoke-on-Trent and had a cup of tea and a cream bun in the cafeteria. Promoter Charles Ochiltree, who was always looking for nicknames for his riders, straightaway decided that I was 'The Cream Bun Kid'.
>
> Years later, when I became a director of Coventry City Football Club, the local newspaper reported my appointment with a splash headline which read 'the return of the Cream Bun Kid'.
>
> I just couldn't get away from it.

Johnnie Reason certainly has no regrets about spending the whole of his speedway career with his home town team, the Coventry Bees. He believes Coventry, through the management skills of Charles Ochiltree and backed by the wealth of owner Alan Sanderson, set standards for the sport which have never been bettered. Coventry staged speedway before the Second World War, at both Brandon Stadium and at the Lythalls Lane greyhound stadium, closer to the city centre. There were moves to develop Brandon in the late 1930s as a multi-sport arena, but these were halted by the hostilities. Johnnie Reason explains:

> At the end of the war, as speedway returned, Brandon and Lythalls Lane were acquired by Sanderson, a mega-wealthy man who owned the Selsdon Park Hotel in Surrey. One of his business partners was Charles Clore, property developer, shipping magnate and philanthropist.
>
> Sanderson was involved in greyhound racing, and he his wife brought over some of the best dogs in the game, particularly from Ireland. When Coventry reopened for speedway in 1948 he was joined by Jack Parker and his wife, who lived at Rugby, quite close to Brandon. They took on as manager Charles Ochiltree, who had been involved at Harringay. That was probably one of the best moves anyone ever made in speedway.

Three fighting Bees. Johnnie Reason (centre) made his debut for Coventry in 1949 at the age of eighteen, a year after fellow Coventrian Derek Tailby (left). When the Bees won Division Two in 1953 the side was strengthened by Reg Duval (right) from Liverpool.

Ochiltree was a wonderful operator, one of the best there has ever been. . . He really got it all together at Brandon. Everything had to be the best, whether it was the riders' machinery or the smartness of the track staff.

Alan Sanderson was a great speedway enthusiast and came to the meetings in a chauffeur-driven Rolls-Royce. He later acquired an interest in Blackbird Road, Leicester, operating as Midland Sports Stadiums, and gave an annual dinner for the Coventry and Leicester teams and their wives at Selsdon Park. We had separate tables decorated with model speedway tracks, complete with bikes.

Johnnie's own speedway career began on a training circuit laid out on the Coventry car park, where Charles Ochiltree encouraged local talent.

We were all motorcycle-mad in those days. As youngsters, myself, Peter Brough and Roy Whitehouse used to scour the back yards and gardens of Coventry for motorcycles left behind when their owners had been called up to the forces. We were all members of a youth club, where we used to do the bikes up and then ride them on a field.

Coventry opened for business in the National League Division Three in 1948, with an initially quite modest crowd, for the era, of around 6,000 people. Despite a fairly unsuccessful side, attendances at Brandon rocketed, to an average of 14,000–15,000. The credit for this success lay primarily with the flair, showmanship and utter professionalism of Ochiltree, who was commended by the Board of Control for the 'dignity and effectiveness' of Brandon's shows, entertaining, in a thirty-meeting season, more than a third of a million people.

The Bees were elevated to Division Two for 1949. The team, largely consisting of riders in the veteran stage – including pre-war star Les Wotton – finished bottom, yet increased the average attendance to 19,000. Ochiltree decided the future lay at least in part in developing local talent, and the eighteen-year-old Reason was part of his plans.

Johnnie had nine matches in the Bees team in 1949, then made the big breakthrough in 1950, when Coventry leapt to fourth place. Reason scored almost 200 points, averaging 7 a match, and appeared in the Britain versus Overseas series on Division Two tracks and in the one-off Scotland v England Test match at Glasgow White City. He was joined in the Bees team by his youth club motorcycle repair colleague Peter Brough and another local boy, Derrick Tailby.

Johnnie maintained his form in 1951 and again in 1952, when Coventry, with another local boy making his debut in the shape of future captain Jim Lightfoot, finished runners-up to Poole. Coventry's turn for the Division Two title came in 1953, and Johnnie was again among the points.

His success, however, was not without its cost. He broke many bones and his back was injured badly when another rider's machine slid into him at Stoke. These injuries, together with marriage and his father-in-law's insistence that he get a 'proper' job hastened his retirement and the start of a successful business career, building up an international haulage company.

Coventry star Johnnie Reason gained international recognition for England in a 66–42 victory over Scotland at Leicester. Reason is pictured (left) in conversation with team-mate Reg Fearman (centre) and Ken McKinlay of Scotland.

Spending a week on a special bed for spinal injuries certainly makes you thing about things. Like many former riders, I still feel the results of some of those injuries today, nearly 60 year later.

Coventry continued to be a successful and well-supported club throughout speedway's so-called dark period in the mid- to late 1950s, and went on to be one of the sport's top venues into the new century, although a dispute with the British Speedway Promoters Association which threatened the track's future was unresolved at the time of going to press. Johnnie Reason has no doubt that the magic of Charles Ochiltree kept the crowds rolling into Brandon when other tracks were closing for lack of support.

Charles was so professional in everything he did and if speedway had possessed a few more people with his management skills and vision for the future I am sure it would be in a stronger position today.

Not that I will every really forgive him for that 'Cream Bun Kid' tag!

Speedway teams often travelled by train in the immediate post-war era, particularly on long tips to Scotland or the South-West of England. The bikes were loaded into the guard's vans and the riders travelled together, with the host track sending a lorry to collect the machines on arrival.

The young Johnnie Reason (left) disliked the nickname of 'Cream Bun Kid' bestowed upon him by promoter Charles Ochiltree (right) but there is no animosity evident in this picture from Brandon Stadium.

In the case of Coventry, who continued to use the railways until well into the 1960s, Johnnie Reason remembers that in his day Charles Ochiltree and his wife Linda travelled first-class, with the riders in third. Arrangements did not always go exactly to plan.

Before setting off on one trip, Jim Lightfoot, who was a particular friend of mine, wanted to see his girlfriend. As my girlfriend worked quite close to Jim's we went off together. Of course, the result was that we missed the train. When we realised it was going to be a close-run thing, Jim said we had better make it look good, so we rode our bikes actually on to the platform at Birmingham New Street station. That got a lot of coverage in the newspapers.

Charles Ochiltree was not actually travelling with the riders that day and we had to telephone him to confess that we had not caught the train. He said we had to get up to Glasgow some way or other or else we would be two men short.

He told us to stay close to a phone. When he rang us back he told us to load the machines on to a van, go to Birmingham Airport, catch a plane for Belfast and then change planes over there for another flight to Glasgow. It was the most roundabout trip either of us ever made to a speedway meeting but it also showed Ochiltree's amazing organisational skills.

CHAPTER EIGHT

1953

Patriotic gestures not enough in Coronation year

S peedway was not sure what to make of prospects for 1953. It was no ordinary year, with the Coronation of Her Majesty Queen Elizabeth II dominating headlines in the early weeks of the season and much time being devoted to planning individual and group celebrations. The event demanded something positive and speedway's response at the highest level was fairly revolutionary. In place of Division One's well-established season-long programme in which each side met each other on four

Speedway joined in the celebrations for the Coronation of Queen Elizabeth II, with a front page featuring a portrait of the young monarch and pictures of riders from the UK and the Commonwealth.

occasions, proceedings were split into two distinct competitions – the Coronation Cup, run on a league basis, and the traditional Division One contest.

The temporary change was a success, but cost Harringay Racers the club's best-ever chance of Division One glory. The Coronation Cup came first, with home and away fixtures between each team. Harringay, the form team of the year, were clear victors, with a 6-point margin over Wembley.

When the focus switched to the Division One competition, Harringay, with an attractive line-up scoring solidly all down the order, again looked likely to take the honours. However, a late run of injuries, particularly the unavailability for two weeks of Split Waterman, halted the Racers' progress to the double and Wembley sneaked in for the club's fifth successive Division One title, with just a point to spare.

When performances over the two separate parts of the season, in the Coronation Cup and the league, were aggregated, Harringay emerged 4 points clear of the Lions. Statistics can lie – the record books largely ignore the Coronation Cup and you will search in vain for a National League title attributed to Harringay. The actual events of 1953 show that the Racers achieved what was at least a moral victory.

Wembley struggled early in the season but then brought off one of the transfer coups so beloved of Sir Arthur Elvin. A significant contributor to Poole's back-to-back championship successes – Division Three in 1951 and Division Two a year later – had been the form of local discovery Brian Crutcher. Elvin paid the Pirates £2,500 for the teenager in May 1953, and another legend was created.

Coronation year also put the emphasis very firmly on the Commonwealth, well represented in speedway with riders from Australia, New Zealand, South Africa and Canada.

In 1952 the patriotic *Speedway News* had recalled that the late King George VI was a motorcycle enthusiast, at one time riding a Harley-Davidson machine. Now it devoted its front page to a portrait of the new queen, surrounded by pictures of riders from the speedway nations over which she was to reign. Great Britain was represented,

The mid-season closure of New Cross was a major blow. Cyril Roger (centre) was still keeping the Rangers ahead of the opposition (Wembley in this case) in the early weeks of the season.

New Cross tried vainly to get Control Board consent to sign Swedish star Olle Nygren as gates slumped in 1953.

inevitably, by Jack Parker, while there could be few arguments about the current World Champion Jack Young having the place of honour for Australia.

Pioneer Wally Kilminster and the *News'* own columnist Trevor Redmond stood for New Zealand, while the now-retired Eric Chitty was the Canadian representative. Canada was actually still represented on UK tracks in 1953, by Mike Tams at Southampton. Roy Bester carried the flag for South Africa, then still both a member of the British Commonwealth and an active speedway nation.

It is probably safe to say that, preoccupied by preparations for the big day, the queen was not daily watching out for Coronation Cup results. Although Prince Philip was at Wembley in 1948 to present the Riders Championship trophy to Vic Duggan, Her Majesty has not to date graced a speedway meeting. Not that she is entirely unaware of a pastime to which, at the time of her accession to the throne, so many of her subjects were addicted. Years later, when she invested World Champion Peter Collins with his MBE and asked what he had done to merit the award, he said he was a speedway rider. The Queen replied, 'Oh, that's the old oval racing, isn't it?' This proves that she must have been aware of speedway at some stage in her long and distinguished reign.

Jim Stenner, not always an optimist, predicted a boom year for speedway in 1953. He was to be proved spectacularly wrong, but hindsight is a wonderful thing. There were twenty-eight starters, nine fewer than there had been for the beginning of 1951 and five fewer than had come to the tapes in 1952. The lower divisions ran a normal league programme in contrast to the top tier, although Division Two added the Queen's Cup to the fixture lists to mark the special year. At the end of the 1952 campaign Cradley had 'merged' with Wolverhampton, with the Wolves stepping up to Division Two. Aldershot dropped out of the Southern League, but Oxford stepped down from the second tier. Although Division One remained constant at ten teams at the start of the season, Division Two shrank from twelve clubs to ten, while the Southern League numbered nine tracks.

Although speedway had already experienced a number of closures, and although in 1953 the sport was still able to support a fairly healthy three-division structure, it really was the year that the post-war boom began to crumble with a vengeance. It was not so much the number of the tracks that closed – just three in fact – but their quality and diversity.

Perhaps the greatest rider of all time made his British debut in 1953. This is believed to be the first UK picture of Ove Fundin, taken in the pits at Rayleigh, where he rode for touring Swedish side Filbyterna.

The first casualty, Liverpool, which withdrew from Division Two in early July 1953, was perhaps the least surprising. Stanley Stadium staged speedway sporadically pre-war, without a great deal of success. Promoter Jimmy Baxter, who was also associated with Southampton and Plymouth, reopened the track for Division Three racing in April 1949, together with manager Gordon Parkins, who went on to achieve considerable success at Norwich in later years. There were several distinctive things about Liverpool. The track was the longest in the country, varying in the post-war period from 430 yards to 446 yards – a staggering 184 yards longer than the shortest circuit in the sport at New Cross – and generally considered to be just too big for close racing. The team, promoted to Division Two in 1951, was nicknamed the Chads, one of the strangest titles the sport has ever known. It was based on a cartoon character called Mr Chad – a bald-headed man with a prominent nose peeking over a wall, with the fingers of each hand clutching the brickwork.

Stanley had plenty of room for spectators, matching the size of the actual track, and initial attendances were promising, culminating in a crowd of 16,474 in the first season. The team, although never successful when it came to winning silverware, was usually an interesting mix of veterans, including pre-war riders like Tommy Allott and leg-trailers Percy Brine and George Newton, and up-and-coming men like Reg Duval, who progressed quickly from novice to top-scorer. The Chads were also notable for their strong South African contingent, including Doug Serrurier, Buddy Fuller and Fred Wills.

The biggest name to be associated with Liverpool was that of future World Champion Peter Craven, who started his career with the Chads as a sixteen-year-old – and a young looking one at that. Craven achieved very little at Stanley, although his subsequent transfer without a fee to Belle Vue attracted some criticism at the time.

Liverpool's withdrawal completed a black week for speedway. Four days before the last meeting at Stanley, Cardiff threw in the towel after a brief, roller-coaster career that reproduced in miniature the up-and-down experience of speedway as a whole in the immediate post-war years. Cardiff, like Liverpool a major port and a sports-mad city, had also staged speedway at intervals throughout the pre-war period, at the White City Stadium. The post-war venue was at Penarth Road, also used for a spell by the equally short-lived Cardiff Rugby League Club. After some training sessions in 1950

The riders are pushed off on parade before a World Championship qualifier at Birmingham. Left to right are Tommy Miller (Glasgow), Maury Dunn (Harringay), Dan Forsberg (of Vargana, Sweden, and Birmingham signing autographs at the fence), Graham Warren (Birmingham), Stig Pramberg (Vargarna), Alan Hunt (Birmingham) and Arthur Payne (Birmingham).

the Cardiff Dragons took their place in Division Three and became an instant success, with reported crowds of up to 20,000 people. So successful was the venue that the Division Three promoters staged their 1951 individual riders championship final at Penarth Road and there was considerable agitation among the fans for promotion, with Division One proclaimed as the eventual destination.

Speedway's perennial problem, in some areas at least, of building and retaining a base of reasonably consistent, long-term, support, raised its head again in the Welsh capital. Cardiff lined up for the track's third season in the 1953 Southern League, but soon discovered that the average attendance in 1952 had dropped by two-thirds to just 3,000. Many disgruntled fans complained that the absence of a formal promotion and relegation system had been a major contributor to the track's downfall. Given the fact that Cardiff had been Southern League runners-up in 1952, but finishing a good 10 points behind Rayleigh, promotion would have been on potential rather than direct merit. As a result of the closure, Wales was to be without speedway for more than a decade.

The third closure – actually the first in terms of date order and by far the most significant – was the demise of New Cross after a Coronation Cup match against Bradford on 10 June had finished in a 42–42 draw. The New Cross withdrawal was,

The World Championship went for a second time to Freddie Williams of Wembley. Second was Split Waterman, with unfancied New Zealander Geoff Mardon taking third spot after a run-off with Olle Nygren.

understandably, reported by the speedway media as a shock of the first order. While it was nothing new for clubs to fold in the lower divisions, in the provinces, London's big five were regarded as the untouchables. New Cross and promoter Fred Mockford claimed direct, unbroken descent from the Crystal Palace team which had competed in the Southern League in 1929. Mockford and his long-time business partner Cecil Smith transferred the Palace team to the Old Kent Road venue for 1934, and from that time onwards the top tier of speedway and the Rangers were synonymous.

New Cross had survived the death of the fans' first hero, Tom Farndon, in 1935 and the Rangers rewarded their loyalty and enthusiasm with a National League Division one championship win in 1938. Other London area tracks had come and gone in the pre-war years, including the initial Southern League champions Stamford Bridge (racing at the home of Chelsea Football Club), Clapton, Lea Bridge, Hackney Wick and the pioneering venue at High Beech. The big five became established with the opening of Harringay in 1934. Although the Racers did not reopen until the second season after the war, for the best part of two decades, war years excepted, London speedway meant racing five nights a week, at Wimbledon, West Ham, New Cross, Wembley and Harringay.

Frequent local derbies, with crowds swelled by visiting fans able to take advantage of the relatively easy cross-city travel in the capital, meant that London speedway was virtually a self-sufficient (and perhaps at times self-satisfied) entity. In some years only Belle Vue and one or two other provincial tracks broke the London stranglehold on the top tier, and the speedway press was often full of complaints about the alleged poor performances of out-of-town teams on the capital's tracks.

The declining crowds of the early 1950s had offered something of an early warning that even London was not protected from speedway's growing problems, particularly the problems at West Ham that resulted in the 1952 takeover by Alan Sanderson. There had been rumours for some time that New Cross was vulnerable, but in the sense that the Old Kent Road closure was the first real crack in the post-war London structure, it was a body blow to a far from confident sport, suffering the effects of a wet summer and the Coronation, which had drastically increased ownership of television sets.

Fred Mockford himself cited many reasons for the closure, including the exceptionally bad weather, the spread of television, and a shortage of money for spending on entertainment outside the home. What Mockford did not seem to take into account was the fact that social histories of the era record that much more of families' disposable income was being spent *inside* the home, not only on TV sets but also on the much wider range of household gadgets and goods now becoming available. Many of the thousands of girls and young women who made up such a significant proportion of crowds at New Cross (and throughout the sport) were now choosing a TV set, a contemporary three-piece-suite and other items, usually paid for through weekly instalments, and once clothes rationing had disappeared, were increasingly fashion-conscious. All of this was siphoning-off the spare cash once spent on a night at the speedway, especially where the purse strings were in female hands.

There is a strong case for suggesting that the increasing influence and economic power of women played a significant but insufficiently recognised role in the decline of popularity of not just speedway but also of cinemas and music halls/variety theatres – another area where Mockford had interests. The decline was not as marked in football, cricket and greyhound racing – the men would find the money to watch their football team whatever; when it came to a choice for the womenfolk between speedway and consumer items however, speedway lost out.

In an echo of many contemporary complaints about the sport, Mockford also believed speedway had become too slick and predictable. He called for a return to the old-style deep cinder tracks, the spectacular leg-trailing style of riding, and for all-star individual events to take precedence over league racing. There was also a feeling that the crowd-drawing potential of individual riders, with Ron Johnson at New Cross perhaps the greatest single example, was often under-estimated. The Rangers did return to National League racing, in 1960 and 1961, when Johnnie Hoskins tried in vain to recapture the old enthusiasm, and there was a disastrous half-season in the Provincial League in 1963. However, the mid-season withdrawal in 1953 really marked the end of an era at the Old Kent Road circuit.

Speedway's renowned inner strength meant that the sport as a whole sympathised with Mockford and with the loyal fans in Liverpool and Cardiff, and then got on with the job in hand. Fittingly for Coronation Year the mother country regained the speedway ashes, with a 2–1 victory over Australia in a curtailed series. Jack Young was still Mr Consistency for the Aussies, but when the series opened, with a 62–46 victory for the men from Down Under at Norwich, the team's trump card appeared to be Ronnie Moore. Moore recorded an impressive 18-point maximum at The Firs, in a one-sided

There were just three England versus Australia Tests in 1953, with England taking the series 2–1. The Lions won 57–51 at Wembley in the Second Test after losing the first match in the rubber at Norwich. The team on the night was, back row, left to right: Dick Bradley, Tommy Price, Charles Ochiltree (manager), Split Waterman and Freddie Williams. Front row: Tommy Miller, Pat Clarke, Brian Crutcher and Eric Williams.

Lions and Kangaroos on the race-jackets had been replaced by national flags. This is the Australian team for the Second Test at Wembley. Back row, left to right: Aub Lawson, Keith Gurtner, Arthur Simcock (manager), Jack Young, Ronnie Moore and Graham Warren. Front row: Arthur Payne, Jack Biggs and Peter Moore.

Wembley won the last of its seven post-war Division One titles in 1953. After a faltering start, management signed Brian Crutcher from 1952 Division Two champions Poole.

encounter in which only home rider Billy Bales returned a double-figure score for England.

The media judged the second Test, at Wembley, to be the best match of the rubber. Split Waterman gave the Lions the perfect start when he beat Jack Young in the first heat, and the encounter was also notable for some inspired team management from Charles Ochiltree of Coventry, making one of his first appearances as an official at the highest level. When Australia pulled away to a 15–9 lead, and it became apparent that some team members were having an off night, Ochiltree had no hesitation in making full use of his impressive reserves, Wembley riders Tommy Price and Eric Williams. The duo scored 27 points between them in England's 57–51 success.

The deciding match was scheduled for Perry Barr, Birmingham, but Australia's hopes were shattered by the non-appearance of Ronnie Moore, reported to have 'met with an accident while on holiday'. The rejuvenated Price top-scored with 14 points for the Lions, well supported by Waterman, Eddie Rigg and local star Alan Hunt, in a 61–47 England victory. Another local hero, Graham Warren, managed just 3 points from his reserve slot.

There was even worse news to follow for Australia later in the year. Ronnie Moore, born in Tasmania but raised in Christchurch, New Zealand, decided that for Test purposes he was to be considered in future as a New Zealander. His decision meant that for the next few seasons, Test series would be labelled as England versus Australasia, featuring both Moore and fellow Christchurch discovery Barry Briggs.

Fred Williams became only the second man to win the World Championship title twice with his success on a rain-soaked surface at Wembley in September, beating the highly fancied Split Waterman and New Zealander Geoff Mardon, not usually recognised as a wet track expert. Williams put his victory down to his extensive grass-track experience and the fact that his preparation had concentrated on starts – again a major factor on a greasy track.

It was just like my grass days – I knew the answers before the skids occurred. I had the break too at the start of most heats, not because I am a Wembley rider – there is no such thing as secret practice on the track – but because I practised starting nearly a thousand times in the Wembley car park. The rider who snaps off first has a 90 per cent chance.

The Belle Vue Aces had their worst season, finishing next to bottom in Division One. Jack Parker was nearing the end of his career and it was also to prove to be the last season at Hyde Road for Louis Lawson, who fractured his skull at the end of the campaign. Back row, left to right: Harry Edwards, Ron Johnston, Jack Parker, Ken Sharples and Louis Lawson. Front row: Peter Craven, Dick Fisher and Bob Fletcher.

In Division Two, 1953 was to prove the last season for some years for Stoke, who withdrew at the end of the campaign. Reg Fearman, who had joined the Potters from West Ham after his national service and was later to promote at Sun Street, leads team-mate Don Potter and Dennis Parker of Leicester, the nephew of Jack and Norman.

Birmingham's Graham Warren won the Midland Riders Championship in 1953. He is pictured with runner-up Len Williams of Leicester (left) and third-placed Eric Boothroyd, a Brummies team-mate.

Close-up action from Old Meadowbank as Monarchs' South African rider Roy Bester leads Len Williams of the visiting Leicester Hunters.

Inter-divisional challenges were popular and Jack Parker and his Belle Vue team attracted a packed crowd to Sun Street, Hanley.

The closure of Halifax gave Bradford a new star in the person of Arthur Forrest. These are the 1953 Bradford Tudors with, left to right, Al Allison, Eddie Rigg, Forrest, Ron Clarke (on machine), Dent Oliver, Bruce Booth (promoter), Wal Morton, Dick Seers, Arthur Wright and Bill Longley.

Back on the domestic scene, Coventry's steady rise to speedway success was capped by the Division Two championship. The Bees established an early supremacy in the division but slumped in August both at home and away, at one stage losing five successive matches.

Contributing factors to a popular success were the steady scoring throughout the order, led by New Zealander Charlie New and the influence yet again of Charles Ochiltree, who according to the *Stenners Annual* handled his team with 'the cool, calculating ruthlessness of a man who meant to win.' Just as with the Test team at Wembley, Ochiltree never hesitated to use his reserves, then as now often the decisive factor in speedway success.

Speedway's legendary ability to shoot itself in the foot from a public relations point of view was again evident in the controversies which dogged the Southern League title race between Rayleigh and Exeter. Both at home and away results were ultimately decided in the committee room rather than on the track.

In an early season encounter Rayleigh lost at home to the Falcons but the result was overturned when the Essex side successfully contended that Exeter had illegally used new Australian star Jack Geran as a reserve. The title came down to a clash between the sides in the West Country at the end of September and again there were wrangles about team composition. Rayleigh raced the match under protest and held the home side to a draw which, however, was enough to give the championship and bonus money to Exeter on race points. The Rayleigh management duly protested to the Control Board and won their case, being proclaimed champions. In December Exeter took their case to the highest level – the Royal Automobile Club – which ordered the Control Board to re-hear the case. Exeter eventually became champions. Speedway as a whole appeared to be the loser.

THERE IN 1953 – *Cyril Roger*

For speedway riders, understandably, it is their on-track successes and the camaraderie of the pits that linger in the memory as the years go by. Cyril Roger had a particularly long and a highly distinguished racing career that brought him England Test caps, team success in the shape of two National League championship medals and two National Trophy successes, and individual glory as winner of the highly prestigious London Riders Championship.

Yet the Kent-born-and-bred former grass-track rider – one of three brothers who tasted top-level speedway – would not deny that one of the defining moments in his own career, and indeed in the post-war history of speedway racing, was the mid-season closure in 1953 of his team, New Cross Rangers.

When New Cross pulled out of National League Division One in June 1953, the decision sent shockwaves through much of the speedway world. Coronation year had been tipped to be a good one for a sport which, although attendances had dipped from their 1949 peak, was still fairly buoyant and optimistic. Above all, at least as far as the speedway authorities and the national media was concerned, speedway still had a top division centred on the core five London tracks, packed with star names and riding at the best-appointed stadia in the land, if not in the world.

Cyril Roger buckled on New Cross colours for the last time in 1953 as the iconic Old Kent Road club withdrew in mid-season.

Shock, however, is not a word that Cyril Roger would use in respect of the New Cross demise. No, he says, firmly, he and the other riders at the Old Kent Road stadium could see it coming, even if the hardcore of fans and the media preferred to pretend that all was well.

The riders could certainly see what was coming, and not just by the way the crowds on the terraces were getting thinner. You could actually sense that the enthusiasm, which at New Cross had been absolutely fantastic, especially among the women fans and the teenagers, had started to wane.

The track struggled on but eventually it was too much for the management. Although speedway was revived on a couple of occasions later on, without much success, the 1953 closure was the real end of New Cross. Cyril Roger, having lived through the boom years at the Old Kent Road track, has no idea why interest fell so dramatically.

Why did the enthusiasm at New Cross, and for speedway as a whole, slump as it did? I really don't know and could not tell you to this day. Fred Mockford, the promoter, blamed all sorts of things, including the very high entertainment tax, television, a wet summer, the concentration on the Coronation celebrations, and the fact that the New Cross team, which was weaker than usual at this stage, was not allowed to sign an overseas rider, the young Swede Olle Nygren.

Cyril Roger, by profession a market gardener in his native Kent, started his speedway career at the Old Kent Road track immediately after the war. He was loaned out by New

New Cross was for a period almost a Roger family business. Cyril (left) is shown here with brother Bert, also an England international, while younger brother Bob also had a spell with the Rangers.

Pictured in action in New Cross colours before the closure of the South London track, Cyril Roger initially moved Norwich.

Cross to Exeter and in 1948 enjoyed double trophy success. He won a Division Three championship medal with the West Country track and took part in enough matches for his parent team to also qualify for a Division One award, in the Rangers' only post-war top-tier title success.

The end of New Cross was not the end of his career by any means, although for the rider personally, as well as for the sport, things were never quite the same ever again. He joined Norwich initially and had spells at Poole, Ipswich and Norwich again, before finishing up with three seasons at Southampton in the early 1960s, culminating in another championship medal with the Saints, in 1962.

Riding at the top of the speedway tree, as part of a New Cross team which enjoyed fanatical support, still resonates with Cyril in the second decade of the new millennium. Subsequent generations of speedway fans have been able to experience for themselves something of the atmosphere of New Cross in its heyday, courtesy of the 1948 feature film *Once a Jolly Swagman*, with the crowd and actions scenes filmed at the Old Kent Road. Even today, on film or videotape, the tension of riders competing in the sport's toughest league, and the fanatical enthusiasm of the thousands of supporters thronging the terraces is palpable.

It *was* tough going in Division One in those days, going out against top riders in every race. Being a top rider was also something to really enjoy. We were very much in the limelight, and the New Cross fans would invite you not only to supporters' club social functions, but also to dinner and to their own homes.

New Cross was undoubtedly special and the Rangers fans were enormously enthusiastic and loyal. When we rode at Birmingham there would be trainloads of supporters going up to the Midlands to follow the team. It was something to savour, never just a question of the money, and you felt really special.

Then, somehow, you could sense that the enthusiasm was slipping away, for whatever reason. Perhaps in the late 1940s the huge crowds had been there because people had been deprived of things by the war. As conditions improved, speedway must have become less important to the people.

As a rider I could see it coming, although I could never work out the actual reason. Speedway has had its good times since then but it has never really been the same, has it, since the London tracks began to fold up?

CHAPTER NINE

1954

Stock car menace casts shadow across tracks

D espite the shockwaves caused by the closures of New Cross, Liverpool and Cardiff during the course of the previous season, speedway entered 1954 with an air of mild optimism. The feel-good factor, sadly, was to prove short-lived. Dark shadows in the form of a riders' strike, an early track closure, and the prospect of damaging competition from an entirely new sport menaced speedway straight from the off.

Jim Stenner, writing the introduction to the new edition of his *Annual*, took a positive line, predicting that 1954 would be a better season than 1953, when 'the Coronation plus wet weather killed gates for a six-week period.'

Forecasting is a difficult business in speedway as in anything else and Stenner was soon left eating his words. The season began (or failed to begin) with a Division Two riders' strike over pay rates, causing the first scheduled meetings at Leicester and Coventry to be called off. Once the dispute was settled it took just two weeks of racing before the first track closure occurred – a bitter blow to speedway's already shaky morale and public image.

In addition to the squabbles between riders and promoters and the spectre of closed tracks, there was another major issue to be faced. On Good Friday, a new sport called stock car racing made its successful British debut at New Cross. Arguments about stock cars and their potentially damaging effect on speedway were to occupy promoters, fans and commentators for weeks on end. The fear was not just that stock cars would tempt many away from speedway's shrinking fanbase. Promoters quickly realised that the cars played havoc with track surfaces, causing extra maintenance expense speedway could barely afford.

Much of the optimism in the weeks before the season began had been prompted by a new league structure. Division One had eight clubs, two less than had gone to the tapes a year earlier, with the loss of New Cross and the decision of Bristol, wooden spoonists in 1953, to voluntarily go down a step after four largely unsuccessful seasons in the top tier.

The Division Two which the Bulldogs rejoined had no fewer than sixteen teams, as the result of a merger with the Southern League. The new second-tier structure was

Speedway shrank in 1954 but top stars Aub Lawson of Norwich (left) and Alan Hunt (Birmingham) still served up the thrills.

widely welcomed throughout the sport, with the prospect it offered of new teams and new riders. The next dark cloud on the horizon appeared north of Hadrian's Wall. For much of the post-war period, Scotland had been a jewel in speedway's crown. A Scotland v England international at Motherwell attracted a reported crowd of 35,000.

Glasgow Ashfield had survived a full season following the loss of Ken Le Breton, but Johnnie Hoskins called it a day at the end of 1952. The other three Scottish tracks all finished in respectable mid-table positions in Division Two in 1953 and seemed on the surface to be reasonably healthy. The truth was rather different. Glasgow Tigers had a strong record at home during Coronation year but crowds were falling at White City. At the end of the season, despite an average attendance of 7,000, the promotion was in trouble.

In his book the *History of the Speedway Hoskins*, a first-person account of life at the heart of speedway during the post-war roller-coaster years, Ian Hoskins revealed:

> When the sums were all completed, we were forced into liquidation. The greyhound company, which owned White City and had for many years played snakes and ladders with our rent, mostly in the upwards direction, decided to run the speedway themselves in 1954.

The Tigers riders belonged to the Hoskins family, and the two main men, Miller and Junior Bainbridge, were sold. Miller stayed in Scotland, moving to Motherwell, while Bainbridge went to Ipswich. A new team was to be built around another exciting new Ian Hoskins discovery, Ken McKinlay.

The new promotion was always on shaky ground and when Coventry visited White City for the first meeting of the new season and won, in front of the track's lowest-ever opening meeting crowd of less than 5,000, the writing was on the wall. Although a local derby against Edinburgh drew a slightly higher attendance, the greyhound company pulled down the shutters.

The threat posed by stock car racing was a major issue in 1954. To rub salt into the wound, the UK's first meeting was at New Cross, a Division One track where speedway had failed.

The once-thriving Scottish speedway scene now crumbled in earnest. Edinburgh was next to go, midway through 1954, and Motherwell closed its doors at the end of the season. There would be no more league racing in Scotland until 1960 and, with the loss of Cardiff in 1953, speedway could no longer claim to be a British, as opposed to an English, sport.

Speedway's fall from grace in Scotland was not the end of the 1954 mid-term closures. Wolverhampton and Plymouth also resigned from Division Two before the season was out. Yarmouth had dropped out before a wheel was turned, after being refused permission to delay their start until the holiday season. Thus it was that a league that had begun with sixteen tracks and such high hopes, finished with just eleven clubs.

Disappearing venues were not speedway's only headline story in the early part of 1954. Both the sport's own magazines and the national and regional press were greatly occupied with the arrival of the stock cars and perhaps the greatest shadow over 1954 was that cast by a large American car, with a railway sleeper for a bumper.

The Good Friday debut of stock car racing down the Old Kent Road attracted a very large crowd – between 26,000 and 30,000 people, depending upon which account you believe, with reportedly many thousands more locked outside the gates. Contemporary reports claimed the local railway station had to put up notices warning passengers not to alight, because they wouldn't be able to get in to the stadium where, a year ago, speedway had folded because of lack of support. *Speedway News* nailed its colours to the mast early on, despite carrying an extensive preview of the New Cross event. The *News* said:

> Any speedway enthusiast, ex-Rangers fans in particular, should wear mourning when attending the new sport. Whether stock cars can be successful or not, nothing can alter the fact that they will be attending the funeral of what was once London's finest track.

The bitterness was evident, but not surprising, given the humiliation speedway had suffered over the mid-season New Cross closure. Stock car racing UK style originated in France, with the Stade Buffalo in Paris, a pre-war speedway venue, staging racing in 1952 and 1953. On a smallish oval circuit, contact was not only allowed, but actively encouraged. Ironically, in view of the furore stock cars were to cause, the New Cross meeting was promoted by a man who had ridden in the pioneering High Beech speedway event of 1928 – Australian circus showman Digger Pugh.

There was considerable irony all-round about the stock car threat. Greyhound stadia in London and throughout the provinces had proved natural homes for speedway in the late 1920s. Now the story repeated itself, with stock cars taking to speed tracks throughout the country as speedway promoters, faced with falling crowds for the bikes, were keen to boost their income.

Stock car racing split speedway people down the middle. For weeks on end the *News* devoted a disproportionate amount of its news space to reports both of the latest track to stage a stock car meeting and the frenzied reactions of speedway's administrators. In May the magazine recorded that the Control Board had issued a statement saying that although it 'did not view with favour' stock car racing on speedway tracks, it was prepared to consider 'limited applications from promoters', proving adequate safeguards were forthcoming to ensure the safety of the track for speedway racing. The Speedway Riders' Association (SRA) told the *News* that it was 'not perturbed', but then promptly banned its members from driving stock cars.

The Speedway Control Board, in truth, had very little say in the matter, as neither it as a body, nor the promoters who it licensed, owned the tracks that were staging stock car racing. Once again, speedway's status as, in the main, tenants rather than owners, told against the sport.

Politics, as ever, reared its head. Although *Speedway News* disliked stock car racing on principal, it was at that time no great admirer of the SRA either. The Association had rejected pay terms for a proposed international series, and its ban on stock car participation was attacked by the magazine as another move by the SRA to 'deny its members additional earnings'.

Despite the ban, many current riders drove stock cars, usually under assumed names, like Johnnie Reason at Coventry. This was with the unofficial blessing of Brandon promoter Charles Ochiltree, who as usual was the calmest of all and one of the few

Many current and former speedway riders drove stock cars, despite a threatened ban, and promoters staged meetings to increase revenue. This is Perry Barr, Birmingham, where drivers included former Brummies captain Phil Hart.

men to realise that if stock car racing was run under controlled conditions, it could act as a useful supplement to the speedway diet and income. Former speedway men also had no hesitation in getting behind the wheel, including men currently licensed as team managers by the Control Board, like Wal Phillips of Harringay, Phil Hart of Birmingham and Cyril 'Squib' Burton of Leicester.

Before the end of May stock cars were spreading their wings out of London, with a reported crowd of 38,000 at Odsal, where former speedway star Oliver Hart drove a car. Glasgow White City started featuring stock car racing and the new sport was introduced to other closed tracks, including Long Eaton.

In what must have seemed the last straw to many London speedway loyalists, the front page of *Speedway News* for the 2 June edition advertised the gala opening three days later of stock car racing at Green Lanes. A rumour soon spread that Harringay's league matches were to be switched to New Cross, in order to free up the Racers' stadium, which had a much bigger capacity than the Old Kent Road arena, for stock cars. This did not in fact happen, but Harringay embraced stock cars with enthusiasm, at a time when the track's speedway gates, the lowest in Division One, were falling. Harringay Stadium's owners, the Greyhound Racing Association, directly promoted speedway. The Racers management embraced a tried and trusted speedway formula for shortening a season, while at the same time fulfilling its obligations to the National League. Double-header matches were run, with the result that Green Lanes saw its last 1954 speedway meeting on 18 August, a month before the usual finishing point.

It was to be the last-ever league match at the track. Harringay later staged a Cavalcade of Speed meeting, including speedway, the 1960 Provincial League Riders Championship, and the first ever Internationale, but the Racers as a team were out of business, never to return – the second major blow in two seasons for London.

In the end, the hysteria generated died away. At Coventry, Charles Ochiltree ran Saturday evening stock car meetings on a monthly basis, when the Bees were away, boosting income. Stock cars at Brandon were run with the same efficiency and sense of showmanship as speedway and, unlike at many tracks, the two sports have run side by side without problems ever since.

The Hoskins family also took to stock car promoting, Ian at Glasgow and for a while at Motherwell, with Johnnie enjoying particular success at Harringay. Green Lanes was eventually given a tarmac surface, effectively ruling out speedway, and was a stock car world championship venue before the stadium was eventually sold for the inevitable redevelopment.

Had the stock car paranoia continued, it would have been an injustice, for there were many speedway highlights in 1954, including the first appearances in a Wembley World Championship final of three future champions and legends of the sport, in the form of Barry Briggs, Peter Craven and Ove Fundin.

With riders like Jack Young, Fred Williams, Split Waterman and others now the established generation and the pre-war and immediate post-war stars rapidly disappearing from the scene – 1954 saw the retirement of Jack Parker – it was certainly time for the young guns to make their mark.

Wimbledon's teenage sensation of 1950, Ronnie Moore, matured fast and won the 1954 World Championship title, ahead of Brian Crutcher (centre) and Olle Nygren.

Ronnie Moore's smooth style and consistently high points returns helped guide Wimbledon to a first-ever Division One championship in 1954, ending Wembley's run of success.

The final was won by Ronnie Moore, still only twenty-one years old, although a fixture in Division One since his 1950 debut for Wimbledon. Runner-up was Brian Crutcher, just twenty, but making his third successive World Final appearance. Another sign of the times was the first podium appearance of a rider from the European continent, in the form of the much-in-demand twenty-three-year-old Olle Nygren, an all-round motorcyclist and a legend in his Swedish homeland.

Despite the disruption caused by the short-lived strike, the domestic speedway season had got off to an encouraging start around the country. *Speedway News* did a review of Easter attendances but, as was usually the case, these were rounded-up approximations, with claims of 25,000 at Belle Vue, 19,000 at Odsal and at Division Two Ipswich, and 8,000 at Edinburgh. A more detailed and perhaps more accurate figure of 13,324 was reported from Odsal for the home team's May RAC Cup win over Wimbledon.

Birmingham, minus Graham Warren, slumped to the foot of Division One, despite the brilliance of Alan Hunt and a good blend of youth and experience. Pictured left to right on the back row are Eric Boothroyd, Arthur Payne, Harry Bastable, Ron Mountford and Ron Barrett. In the front row are Ivor Davies, Les Tolley and Alan Hunt.

The style that was to win Peter Craven (centre) the title of the 'Wizard of Balance' was still developing in 1954 and this shot shows a more conventional cornering technique.

Bristol stepped down a division in 1954. The Bulldogs gave their fans some consolation by immediately winning the Division Two championship. The small and tricky Knowle stadium track again provided considerable home advantage.

When Bristol stepped down to Division Two, most of the Bulldogs' team stayed loyal too, including England international Dick Bradley.

If track closures and the advent of stock car racing had not proved big enough shocks for the speedway world in 1954, the destination of the Division One championship was also a surprise, if in many ways a welcome one. Wembley had previously won seven out of the eight post-war titles, including five in a row in the period 1949–53 period.

Now the dominance was ended, by an attractive Wimbledon team with a strong Dominions element, including Australian veteran Bill Longley, Ronnie Moore, Barry Briggs, Peter Moore – a bargain basement signing from Long Eaton in 1952 – and Geoff Mardon, together with locally developed riders such as England international Cyril Brine and up-and-coming youngsters like Reg Trott, Cyril Maidment and Irishman Don Perry.

The Division Two survivors were headed by Bristol, with the championship title, last seen at Knowle in 1949, some compensation for the loss of top-tier status. Despite the much-vaunted merger between Division Two and the Southern League for the 1954 season, the campaign did also see a third tier, in the shape of the new Southern Area League (SAL). At the most semi-professional, with very low pay rates, the SAL began the season with six tracks. Rye House, once Wembley's training centre and British speedway's most famed developer of young talent, won the championship.

Runners-up were the California Poppies, based at Wokingham in Berkshire, which quickly became a focus for hopefuls from Wimbledon, including future international Bob Andrews, Tommy Sweetman and Gil Goldfinch.

A bright spot in 1954 was the formation of the Southern Area League, designed to give match opportunities to novices. This action shot from California, near Reading, illustrates the primitive safety measures.

Original California girls? Southern Area League riders were paid very little but had their compensation in the shape of some local bathing beauties at one match in 1954.

Ringwood, in the New Forest, were in third place, with Northamptonshire-based Brafield fourth, followed by Eastbourne, enjoying a return to league racing for the first time since winning the initial Division Three championship in 1948. The sixth member of the SAL, Aldershot, somewhat blotted the new league's copybook by resigning mid-season.

Southern Area League tracks were rough and ready, with photographs often illustrating just the flimsiest of barriers between the crowd and the racing bikes. For riders based in the south and the Midlands they provided opportunities for competitive racing that were becoming harder and harder to find as tracks in the two top divisions disappeared. The position was by no means as positive in the north of England. Stoke's closure at the end of 1953 left just Division One Bradford and Belle Vue carrying the flag north of the Trent. There was a training track at Newton Heath, riders used the famous Ainsdale Sands, and Belle Vue staged its famous second half 'Bubble Bounce' event for juniors. This was named after a fairground novelty ride and probably reflected the tendency of some of the novices to be bounced out of the saddle and on to the shale.

Out of work former league riders took part in unlicensed 'pirate' meetings at Long Eaton in September 1954. Although some used assumed identities, former Archer Johnnie Jones, now with Brafield, rode in his own name. The result was a Control Board ban, causing him to miss the SAL Riders championship final (eventually won by the future Southampton rider Alby Golden).

It was not just the juniors who were finding rides difficult to guarantee, as the remaining tracks found themselves with a surfeit of experienced men. Reg Fearman, a heavy scorer for Stoke and for Leicester, recalls:

> With the closure of the tracks in Scotland and the north of England, team places were getting hard to keep. That is why I left for New Zealand at the end of 1954. Leicester, where I was riding at the time, had signed Ken McKinlay from White City and Roy Bester from Edinburgh when those tracks closed during the season and I could see the writing on the wall.
>
> Tommy Miller had held out against moving south but when the last Scottish track at Motherwell closed at the end of 1954 he signed for Coventry. His team-mates Gordon McGregor and Ron Phillips came to Leicester and I was aware that I was dropping down the order.

Altogether, there was a great deal of uncertainty about the future structure of speedway in October 1954, as the tracks closed down for the winter break. Ironically, given the optimism with which journalist and editor Jim Stenner had greeted 1954, one important decision had already been taken. For the first time since speedway restarted in 1946, there would be no *Stenners Annual* in the spring of 1955.

THERE IN 1954 – *Bob Andrews*

The endless wrangling about whether or not stock car racing would deliver the death blow to speedway rather went over the heads of Bob Andrews and most of his fellow young hopefuls in 1954. Although speedway tracks were closing or threatening to close all over Britain, Bob and many others were ignoring the pessimists and doing their best to break into a sport which, they confidently believed, had a future.

Southern novices were really boosted by the formation in 1954 of the Southern Area League, where young riders could learn their trade in organised, safe but competitive conditions, and, at the same time, entertain sizeable numbers of spectators.

Bob graduated from cycle speedway with Lea Valley Knights to the California Poppies. The team name that fascinated speedway supporters came from the track's location at Little California in England, near Wokingham in Berkshire. In the 1950s the area had a lake, a funfair, holiday camp and, from 1951 to 1957, a speedway track. Today it is a country park, which stages reunions of Poppies riders. Bob was talent-spotted by former rider Mick Mitchell at Rye House (where he paid £5 for a day's training on a borrowed bike). Mitchell made an urgent phone call to Wimbledon promoter Ronnie Greene, saying:

> Hop down quick, I'm at Rye House. I've never seen such a stylist first time out on a speedway bike.

Wimbledon signed Bob, found him a machine and loaned him for experience to California. He settled in to a team which over the years included several riders who made a mark with Wimbledon and other teams in senior speedway, including Jim Tebby, Gil Goldfinch, Ron Sharp, Eric Hockaday and Roy Bowers. In the first year of the SAL, the Poppies finished runners-up to Rye House. Bob explained:

Although teams were collapsing all over the place in the mid 1950s I still wanted to race speedway. I suppose that, moneywise, I was doing it for next to nothing, as were all the other riders in the Southern Area League.

As far as I can remember you had to get a maximum in the match *and* win the second half at an SAL meeting to collect between £5 and £6. To a youngster that was quite a lot of money at the time.

Although Mick Mitchell had been excited when he first saw me, and Wimbledon gave me a contract, I was just 'nibbling' at racing in 1954 and 1955. I got my break in 1956, when Ron How broke his wrist.

The Southern Area League was a stepping-stone to stardom for Bob Andrews.

Bob grabbed his big chance with both hands and in his first team outing for the Dons won a heat from the back and picked up a third place behind a team-mate. He was a key member of the Wimbledon team for nine years, during which time the Dons won the National League title five times to add to two further titles achieved before he broke into the side.

With Ronnie Moore, Barry Briggs, Geoff Mardon, Cyril Brine, etc, Wimbledon were a fearsome team and a lot of the other sides, particularly at Plough Lane, were beaten before the match started.

I had a good season when I was racing as partner to Ronnie – as I was a 'gater' he would push me home. Then in 1957 I was paired with Barry Briggs, who in my view was a very selfish rider. I was still making the gate but he would literally push me out of the way to pass me – so much for team riding.

I had more or less decided to give it all away but then I had a chance to race in South Africa, which really boosted my career. I got third place in the South African Championship, ahead of Ove Fundin, and when I came back to the UK I really started moving.

Moving was what Bob did quite a bit of in the 1960s. After a disagreement with Ronnie Greene he made up his mind to leave Plough Lane. The National League and the Provincial League were in conflict in 1964 and the Provincials were running outside the jurisdiction of the Control Board.

Bob was the only major rider to take the plunge and decide to ride 'black' for Wolverhampton. It led to him being sued in the High Court by Wimbledon and also to his team-mates sending him to Coventry for a spell – and not in the speedway sense.

Bob Andrews in action at California in the Southern Area League.

The California Poppies, 1954. Left to right are Fred Milward (team manager), Peter Mould, Jimmy Gleed, Ron Sharp (on machine), Gil Goldfinch, Fred Babcock, Jim Webb and Jack Griffin (secretary). Kneeling are (left) Bob Andrews and (right) George Baker.

When the two leagues joined forces in 1965 he got his move to Wolverhampton, but at the end of that season decided to concentrate on his new love – New Zealand. After becoming a naturalised Kiwi, he represented New Zealand in international matches (he had previously ridden in Tests for England), and won the NZ individual championship in February 1966, with a 15-point maximum. A career highlight was winning the World Pairs Championship in Stockholm in 1969, partnering Ivan Mauger.

Bob returned to British speedway in 1968 and spent four seasons back in the Black Country at Cradley Heath, with one campaign at Hackney neatly sandwiched in between. Today he keeps in touch with the veterans scene in New Zealand, occasionally rides a speedway bike, and is closely involved with the speedway ambitions of his young grandson Bradley.

CHAPTER TEN

1955

Sea air fails to revive track fortunes

British speedway hoped a breath of sea air would provide a much needed tonic in 1955. In the event, the almost immediate failure of the first new league track for several years simply kicked sand in the face of the sport's optimists and cost its promoters a good deal of money. The mid-season closures which bedevilled the 1954 season continued into the autumn and winter of 1954/55, with the confirmation of the expected closure of Harringay and the regrettable end of league speedway in Scotland, with the withdrawal of Motherwell.

The authorities seemed powerless to halt the decline in the number of National League tracks, which continued to be steady if still not exactly catastrophic. The twenty-three starters in the spring of 1954, already thinned out by the four mid-season withdrawals, dropped to just seventeen survivors when the dust settled and promoters began to plan for 1955.

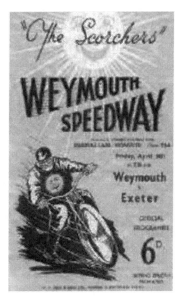

The closure trend was surprisingly reversed with an application for Division Two membership from an entirely new track in the south coast seaside resort of Weymouth. The Dorset track was the first entirely new venue to appear in National League racing since Ipswich's 1952 Southern League debut. The men behind Weymouth were two local entrepreneurs and an experienced speedway operator in the form of Bill Dutton, who at Exeter in the 1953 season had been involved in one of those situations which over the years have, with some justification, exposed the sport to media ridicule.

Speedway looked to the seaside in 1955 for a revitalising tonic, as Weymouth became the first track to join the league set-up since Ipswich in 1952.

There were plenty of experienced riders available when Weymouth made a bid to establish National League speedway in the resort, including Danny Dunton, formerly of Harringay and a World Finalist in 1950, who was an ever-present during the team's brief existence.

Dutton was for a while team manager of both Exeter and Cardiff. When *Speedway News* pointed out the farcical nature of the irreconcilable roles, Dutton decided that Cardiff, then riding high with large crowds and Division One ambitions, was the best bet. It hardly proved to be a wise move, as Exeter won the Division Three title that year while Cardiff threw in the towel. Such was the train of events that brought Dutton to the new Wessex Stadium in Weymouth, which had held a licence for greyhound racing since the autumn of 1952. The first speedway meeting was held in August 1954, when reigning World Champion Freddie Williams was guest of honour.

The Scorchers, as the Weymouth team was named, raced a series of challenge matches that year, using guest riders, and the response was sufficient to prompt the management to apply successfully for a Division Two place for 1955.

With so many tracks having closed, it was not too difficult for Weymouth to attract a reasonably strong-looking team, with former Stoke favourite Ken Adams as captain, backed up by Australian Ernie Brecknell, and former World Finalist Danny Dunton.

Things started well, with a 52–44 home win over Exeter, but poor results, bad weather and dipping crowds led to closure after just six home meetings, the final one ending in a heavy defeat at the hands of Rayleigh.

Holiday resorts and areas and speedway have not always been successful bedfellows, usually due to the lack of population during the spring and autumn periods of the season. The most notable exception, Poole, is in itself a largish town and is on the edge of a considerable conurbation, including Bournemouth.

Eastbourne, situated in the countryside some miles outside the fair-sized Sussex resort, staged speedway from almost the start of the sport in Britain, but in pre-war days and throughout most of the 1950s it was as a Sunday afternoon training track, apart from the financially unsuccessful 1947 season when the team won the new Division Three in 1947.

On the east coast, Yarmouth's final National League season had been in 1953, when crowds had been poor outside the relatively short peak holiday season. The management at the Norfolk track made it clear that continuing to race in 1954 was dependent upon the Control Board allowing the club to wait until well into the season before opening its doors. Permission was refused, and that was the end of the venue until 1959, when the short season raced in the Southern Area League proved more acceptable than a March-October span.

Over the years there had been several unsuccessful attempts to establish speedway in Blackpool, not only a sizeable town with a highly successful football team in the 1950s, but also arguably Britain's premier seaside resort. Neighbouring Fleetwood was only marginally successful.

The failure of Weymouth was a disappointment to all those hoping to see speedway sustain reasonable numbers in its two National League divisions, but the fact that what was clearly a considerable gamble ultimately failed was not a huge surprise. The other mid-season closure in 1955 was much more disturbing.

Bristol is one of those cities where one feels speedway should be a permanent fixture. In reality, the sport in the capital of the west has had a chequered history, both pre- and post-war. Knowle Greyhound Stadium was the home of speedway in Bristol from 1928 to 1960, managed in the late 1930s by future Wimbledon promoter Ronnie Greene. Open licence meetings were staged in 1946 and Bristol joined Division Two the following season. The moderate success of the first term back was followed by a 1948 championship win, marred by the controversial promotion of runners-up Birmingham.

Bristol had to win another Division Two title in 1949 before being elevated and this saw the start of a perhaps never entirely comfortable spell at the highest level of speedway. Bristol's mix of veterans such as Geoff Pymar and new young stars like Dick Bradley usually ensured respectable results and league placings, but, once again, there was often controversy surrounding Knowle.

At least one opportunity to stage a Test match against Australia was turned down by the management, which felt that capacity and facilities at Knowle were insufficient. The track's location well out of the city also told against it when a local bus strike badly hit crowd levels.

After keeping their heads above water both on and off the track for three seasons, Bristol finished bottom in Division One in 1953 and decided to return to the second tier. Championship success at that level the following season was not enough to arrest the slide, resulting in the mid-season pull-out in 1955.

On the Test match scene, the England v Australasia version was now into its second

Stars on the track, unassuming off it, with a lifestyle very different to that of today's Grand Prix stars. Aub Lawson (left) and Harry Edwards pictured at Norwich.

Norwich were originally allocated Australian Test star Jack Biggs for 1955. Biggs failed to arrive for the Stars' first meeting and eventually signed for West Ham.

season. Australia's glory years of 1951 and 1952, with 4–1 series wins over the old enemy on English tracks, now seemed very distant. Throughout the rest of the decade, England was to prove triumphant over the combination of Aussies and Kiwis and 1955 produced a 4–2 series win for the Lions to follow the 3–0 1954 whitewash.

Australasia made an encouraging start to the series, winning 67–39 at Wimbledon, where Ronnie Moore registered an 18-point maximum on his home track, well supported by Jack Young, Peter Moore and Barry Briggs. England levelled matters at Wembley, inspired by Fred Williams and Brian Crutcher, with only Young providing much opposition, but the men from Down Under fought back with a commanding 66–42 victory at West Ham, with both Young and Ronnie Moore registering maximums.

When the series headed for the provinces, England took control, with straight wins at Odsal, Birmingham and Norwich. The deciding factor was the absence of Ronnie Moore for the final two Tests. Barry Briggs was inconsistent throughout the series and most of the supporting cast, including Aub Lawson and Jack Biggs, struggled throughout. Young, not surprisingly, was by far the highest scorer on either side, with 83 points.

England, as usual, pursued a 'horses for courses' policy, which sometimes worked, sometimes failed. Brian Crutcher, who rode in four of the six Tests, was the highest Lions scorer, with 61 points. England's international success extended to the World

All was not well again behind the scenes at West Ham, saved from closure by millionaire Alan Sanderson in 1952 but struggling again by 1955. Despite the presence of former World Champion Jack Young (left) and England's latest overnight sensation, Gerry Hussey, West Ham were bottom of Division One.

Proudly holding a trophy that threatened to dwarf his small stature, Peter Craven crowned his meteoric rise to fame with the World title in 1955.

New Zealanders played an increasingly dominant role in British speedway as the 1950s progressed. In this Belle Vue versus Wimbledon National League match, Australian-born but Christchurch-raised Ronnie Moore (left), now preferring to ride as a Kiwi, leads Aces' Ron Johnston from Dunedin, with Moore's team-mate Cyril Brine in the background.

When Norwich signed Ove Fundin in June 1955, not even the most optimistic Firs stadium fan could have foreseen the role the red-haired Swede would play both for the Stars and in world speedway over the next decade. Fundin (centre) is pictured before an early appearance at Wembley, with Norwich team-mates Billy Bales (left) and Phil Clarke.

The classic Fundin style was in evidence from his early days with Norwich. Ove holds the line at the Firs against Ronnie Moore of Wimbledon, with team-mate Phil Clarke in the background.

Championship, where Peter Craven lifted the title at Wembley, ahead of Ronnie Moore and Barry Briggs.

Domestically, Wimbledon won a second successive Division One title, with a Craven-inspired Belle Vue recording their best position since 1951, just 2 points behind. Poole, runners-up in Division Two to Bristol in 1954, took the title ahead of Coventry, while Rye House again won a Southern Area League which was reduced to just four sides when Ringwood resigned in mid-season.

Norwich, beaten finalists in 1954, when they lost to Wembley, became only the second provincial side to lift the National Trophy (Belle Vue were the other) when they beat Wimbledon.

The 1955 season marked the debut in the National League of Ove Fundin, two years after first appearing on British tracks with a touring Swedish club side. It is virtually impossible to find much to say that is new about the career of a true legend. Some aspects of that career will seem almost incredible to the modern-day speedway fan. Today riders switch between clubs with monotonous regularity. Jason Crump, three times World Champion in the Grand Prix era, has ridden in three spells for Poole, three spells for Peterborough, in two different periods for Belle Vue, and also for Swindon, Oxford and Kings Lynn. In 50 years' time, which club will claim that Crump was truly one of their own?

Ove Fundin rode for Norwich from his National League debut in 1955 for ten successive seasons, until The Firs stadium closed for redevelopment at the end of the 1964 season. Although he was to figure in later years in the colours of Long Eaton, Belle Vue and Wembley, these were essentially cameo appearances. In the context of speedway in Britain, Fundin's career revolved around Norwich. Small wonder that he was revered by the fans at The Firs, that his is still a household name in Norfolk today, and that he has been formally honoured by the city fathers.

In his native Sweden, his formative years were spent with Filbyterna, with whom he toured the UK. From 1958 to 1971, a long time in speedway terms, he remained a member of the Kaparna club.

Stories surround living legends. One of the best told about Ove Fundin illustrates the fact that, unlike most motorised sports, an interest in the mechanical side is not compulsory in speedway. John Chaplin's acclaimed biography of Fundin confirms the oft-told tale that Ove never owned a speedway bike in Britain, using a machine christened the 'Norwich Track Spare Number Two' during his years with the Stars.

Revered at Norwich, Fundin was often reviled by supporters at away tracks, incensed by his huge success and sometimes critical of his single-minded determination to succeed. Throughout the mid- and late 1950s, at a time when the sport desperately needed to rekindle its early attraction, Ove Fundin and his great contemporaries in the form of Briggs, Craven and Moore, brought the public through the turnstiles in a way few if any individual riders can do today.

In 2011 Ove Fundin retains an affection for speedway and speedway people, but has trenchant views on the state of the sport, views expressed in a later chapter of this book.

Speedway tradition number one – being tossed high in the air by team-mates was *de rigueur* after a rider had enjoyed a successful evening. Here Harry Bastable of Birmingham receives the full treatment from fellow Brummies Ron Mountford (left) and Les Tolley.

Speedway tradition number two – modern health and safety rules would never permit the tractor ride (seen here at California) that for decades was the way to celebrate a speedway victory at all levels of the sport.

THERE IN 1955 – *Harry Bastable*

Throughout speedway's chequered history, the West Midlands has been a veritable hotbed of the sport. Fans of the region's teams, some of the most knowledgeable and loyal to be found anywhere in the game, enjoy the international headliners who flit in and out of the limelight, but seem to reserve some of their greatest affection and respect for their local products, the solid team men who are the backbone of the sport. One of the area's most notable products was (and is) Harry Bastable, one of the relatively few riders who stuck fast to speedway through the thick and thin of the 1950s.

Birmingham-born Harry's career took him to Cradley Heath, Tamworth, Cradley again, Wolverhampton and Birmingham, with a slight diversion eastwards to Leicester as the sport contracted in the mid-1950s. Finally, as a fitting reward for his persistence in the face of trying times for the sport as a whole and for his own career, he returned to Cradley when the good times returned for speedway.

When Harry Bastable graduated from Cradley Heath to Division One Birmingham, the tank of his machine bore the name of his motorcycle business. The Control Board considered this was sponsorship – absolutely taboo at the time – and tried (unsuccessfully) to make Harry remove the offending title.

1955

Harry was a natural when it came to riding a motorcycle, and his National Service years were spent trick riding with the Royal Artillery display team. When he was eventually demobbed, he joined a civilian display team and took up grass-track racing, scrambling and trials riding.

As a time-served carpenter earning good money at Dunlop in Birmingham, he was at first reluctant when offered a speedway trial at Cradley. Persuaded to at least have a go, he impressed, despite wearing borrowed leathers and boots. A complete stranger to speedway, he didn't even realise he would need a steel shoe to slide the bike.

You had to provide everything yourself in those days, unlike today with all the sponsorship in the sport. As my career developed I started a motorcycle business, called Speedway Motors. When I painted the name on the tank of my bike, I got hauled up in front of the Speedway Control Board in London and told sponsorship wasn't allowed. I argued that it was my own business and won my point.

Midlands speedway supremo Les Marshall, promoting Division One Birmingham and Division Two Cradley, advised Harry to switch initially to the Brummies chief's new Division Three interest at Tamworth. Harry gained vital experience at the Staffordshire track but was back at Cradley in 1951, proving a solid scorer.

His career really took off at Dudley Wood in 1952, when he topped the scorers list, with 355 points from forty-four matches, and was described in the *Stenners Annual* for the following year as having shown 'brilliant form' throughout the season.

Sadly, falling crowds meant that Cradley 'merged' with Black Country rivals Wolverhampton for 1953 and Harry moved with his team-mates to Monmore Green. He had not been forgotten, however, by Les Marshall, and in addition to riding for the Wolves, he made his Division One debut for Birmingham during the season. He had the best part of five seasons at Perry Barr, more than holding his own in a team including fellow Midlanders Alan Hunt and Ron Mountford, South African Doug Davies and Eric Boothroyd. Perhaps his best season was 1955, when the highlights included twelve paid 13 points from five rides against Norwich, followed by a further haul of 12 points against Poole.

In 1956 he scored a paid maximum for the Brummies in an international challenge match against a strong Polish team. When Birmingham started the 1957 season reeling from the double blow of the death of Alan Hunt in South Africa, and the absence of other riders suspended for riding illegally in that country, Harry kept a team place, but his form dipped. He considered retirement, even before Birmingham's mid-season closure, but was talked into moving to Leicester for a three-season spell. In those challenging times for speedway, there was hot competition for team places and, in 1959, Harry dropped out of the Hunters team. Even then, he played a major role in Leicester's success in the National Reserve league, in which they were joint champions with Midlands rivals Coventry.

Harry's first and greatest speedway love was Cradley, and when the Heathens reopened in 1960 in the new Provincial League, he asked for a move. Because of his

The distinctive, seemingly perfectly relaxed Bastable style is in evidence as Harry heads opponents from a Polish touring team at Perry Barr in 1956.

Speedway riders usually needed another job or a business interest in the mid-1950s. This highly evocative shot shows Harry Bastable in the doorway of his Speedway Motors concern.

Division One experience, the Control Board took some persuading, but when he did return to Dudley Wood, it was to considerable success and great popularity with the fans.

> My speedway career is really about Cradley. When you are on the side of the Black Country people, you are one of them and they love you. The Cradley supporters were fanatical and the atmosphere there was incredible.

Why did Harry keep going throughout the 1950s when other riders were quitting the sport in droves?

> I was going up to race in Scotland one time, it was a sunny day, a clear road, I was getting travelling expenses and I thought to myself, I'm getting paid to travel and ride and do something I would do for nothing. When I rode grass-track I had to pay the clubs to enter a meeting.
>
> Speedway was not about the money – it was, for me at least, about pure enjoyment. Some people climb mountains or go down potholes, which I could never do. Speedway was my thing.

CHAPTER ELEVEN

1956

Clinging on to a fast-fading sense of glory

Despite a good deal of pressure from Division Two promoters, with the always realistic Charles Ochiltree in the forefront, speedway retained its two-division format and some semblance of former glory for 1956. With fourteen tracks spread equally between Divisions One and Two, the sport had edged back closer to the size and structure of the post-war revival year of 1946. Significantly, a decade later, only half of the venues that had revived the sport after the war were still operating.

Division Two champions Poole were promoted in 1956, allowing Division One to remain viable. Pirates skipper Ken Middleditch (right) and his team-mates had experience riding on tracks like Belle Vue in the National Trophy.

Poole were strengthened for their first season in Division One by the signing of riders like Cyril Roger, seen here being welcomed to Wimborne Road by Pirates captain Ken Middleditch, and Jack Biggs, who came from defunct West Ham.

The winter of 1955/56 saw the closure of West Ham, another blow for the dominance of London and big city speedway. The sport's geographical boundaries shrank even further when Exeter followed fellow westerners Bristol and Weymouth and closed the gates.

Although many promoters supported a merger into one big league for 1956, there was a feeling that the two-division structure would endure as long as Wembley survived and there were enough tracks to form a viable top tier. Championing the two-division structure, Wembley was still able to point to matches against tried and tested traditional top-tier rivals like Wimbledon and Belle Vue.

The tracks that had managed to break the virtual London/Manchester monopoly and force their way into Division One in the post-war era, through a combination of on-track success and large spectator capacity – Bradford, Birmingham and Norwich – had been accepted by the Wembley management and supporters as reasonably worthy opponents, if not on a par from a crowd-pulling point of view as the now-defunct New Cross, Harringay and West Ham. The six members of the top tier remaining after the departure of the Hammers were boosted by the promotion of Division Two champions Poole. The days of arguments over promoting smaller clubs were long gone as the

By the time West Ham closed to speedway in autumn 1955, Eric Chitty had long retired. This portrait of one of the Hammers' greatest-ever stars and personalities serves to illustrate the graceful sweep of the huge double-deck main grandstand at Custom House, designed by the legendary architect of many iconic stadia, Archibald Leitch.

Although no-one realised it at the time, 1956 was to be Wembley's last season as a permanent fixture in the British league structure, although the Lions were revived for a brief spell in the 1970s. The 1956 team was, back row, left to right: Ray Cresp, Brian Crutcher, Tommy Price (on machine), Split Waterman, Mike Broadbank and Eric French. Kneeling are (left) Trevor Redmond and (right) Brian Hanham.

Birmingham fans were also seeing their final full season of league speedway for many years. This 1956 National Trophy action shot from Perry Barr's still well-populated terraces sees Brummies rider, South African Doug Davies, driving around the outside of Wembley's Ray Cresp and Trevor Redmond, with Ron Mountford at the rear.

surviving giants settled for a pragmatic approach. This left the remaining Division Two tracks to make the best of the smallest second tier the sport had known since 1946.

West Ham, second only to Wembley in crowd-pulling potential in the glory years of the late 1940s, had survived a scare in 1952 and had lost a good deal of their lustre by the end of 1955. The track's closure was nonetheless another real body blow to speedway. The Hammers had been innovators and headline-makers of a high order and everything about the place was big. The full quarter-mile speedway circuit – reduced to 415 yards in 1954 – was one of the longest in the country and was built inside the longest greyhound track in Britain, at 562 yards.

Opened in July 1928, West Ham Stadium had an architectural importance unmatched by any speedway/greyhound venue. Its impressive stands, one with two tiers capable of housing almost half the nominal capacity of 100,000, was designed by Archibald Leitch, the leading sports ground architect of the era, responsible for football grounds including Liverpool's Anfield.

The demise of the Hammers served to illustrate that speedway, unlike virtually every other sport, was in the mid-1950s almost wholly dependent on turnstile income, with sponsorship still far away. Alan Sanderson may have been an enthusiast, but he was not prepared to lose money for long. Promoters needed to show at least a reasonable return, while stadium landlords – usually greyhound companies – always made it quite clear that the dogs were their number one priority. There was to be a long interval, during

One of British speedway's fraternal trios broke up in 1956 when Freddie Williams, pictured (centre) with brothers Eric (left) and Ian, retired in June. Freddie was a Wembley rider for his entire career.

which time speedway genuinely prospered once more, before the decline of the 1990s and the emergence in the sport of promoters who have made their money from other activities before becoming involved in speedway and are, in the words of Ian Hoskins, primarily benefactors rather than business men.

While the end of the sport at Custom House was bitterly regretted, speedway yet again shrugged its shoulders, made yet another call on the deep well of survival skills it had developed, and got on with the job of entertaining a more concentrated yet still sizeable fanbase.

The Southern Area League was also having membership problems, and with Brafield calling it a day before the start of the 1956 season, it was only made viable through the creation of a homeless side called, appropriately enough, Southern Rovers, which rode its 'home' fixtures on the three other tracks.

The England v Australasia series continued, but with just three Tests, all in the provinces. Although Bradford and Birmingham were established Test match venues, England's 57–51 win at Poole was a first for the Dorset venue, which only five years earlier had hosted nothing better than Division Three speedway. The series resulted in a 3–0 victory for England, although two of the matches at least were closely contested.

With Jack Young (temporarily) retired, Australasia relied heavily on two New Zealanders – Barry Briggs a Kiwi by birth and Ronnie Moore by adoption. Brian Crutcher was England's top scorer over the series, although the only rider on either side to score a maximum was Alan Hunt, on his home track at Birmingham.

The other international headlines of 1956 reflected the way that European countries, in Eastern Europe and Sweden in particular, were playing catch-up with England and the Commonwealth.

Ove Fundin, who had made his debut in Britain for a Swedish touring team in 1953, made 1956 a memorable year for his homeland. He not only became the first rider from the European continent to win the World Championship, but also led the Swedish

Above left: Ove Fundin became the first European rider to win the World Championship.

Above right: The first England–Sweden Test series was staged and Sweden won the series 2–1 with wins at Wembley and Wimbledon. A reported crowd of 9,352 saw the Lions win at Norwich, despite the best efforts of home star and series top scorer Ove Fundin, seen here leading the field.

Tracks in the south were more adept at surviving than their northern counterparts. This is the Rayleigh 1956 line-up of, left to right, Pete Lansdale, Les McGillivray, Alan Smith, Arthur Atkinson, John Fitpatrick, Jack Unstead and Maurice McDermot. Gerald Jackson is on the machine.

Wimbledon promoter Ronnie Greene had a policy of encouraging young talent, which paid off as the Dons became the dominant side in Division One of the National League. Pictured at Plough Lane is one of the Don's young hopefuls, Reg Trott.

national side to a 2–1 series victory over a full England team, with victories at Wembley and (by a 1-point margin) at Wimbledon. England's only success was, ironically, on Fundin's home circuit at Norwich, where the Swede dropped points in his fifth ride to the best British pairing of Ken McKinlay, who scored 17 points, and the Lions' series highest scorer, Brian Crutcher.

The Swedish success was a blow to British prestige, as apart from Fundin and Olle Nygren, the team was mostly composed of unknown quantities. The Scandinavian country's dominance was underlined when they entertained England in late September and October and won all three matches in the series.

On the home front Wimbledon made it a hat-trick of Division One victories, and recorded a double by also capturing the National Trophy. Unfashionable Swindon won the track's first-ever championship with a 1-point victory margin over Southampton in Division Two – a portent of even greater things to come for the Wiltshire side. Rye House, for the third successive season, won the Southern Area League.

Despite the declining number of tracks, speedway was still claiming a place at the top table of British sporting activity. In the mid-1950s the *Eagle* comic sold almost a million copies at its peak and the associated annual, published in time for Christmas sales, was also very popular. The author's interest in speedway was largely driven by an article by the late Cyril J. Hart, a well-known speedway journalist based on the south coast of England. 'The Lure of Speedway' appeared in the *Eagle* with some excellent

A humble beginning for a future superstar. When the seventeen-year-old Ivan Mauger first came to England in 1957/58 to ride for Wimbledon, he found the going difficult at Plough Lane. He also rode at Southern Area league tracks Rye House and Eastbourne. He is pictured (centre) in the Eastbourne pits in 1958 with fellow riders including Malcolm Reading (left) and Clive Hitch (second from the left). Mauger went on to win the World Championship a record six times in the 1960s and '70s.

History in the making – part of the front cover of the programme for the last National League match at Wembley. Norwich won a tight match by 43 points to 41 on 30 August 1956.

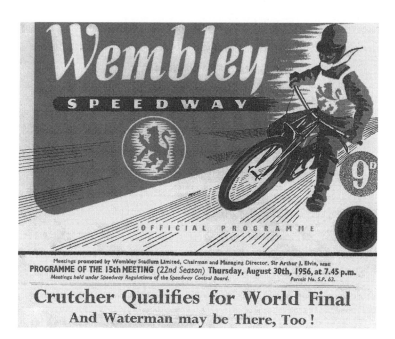

Wembley

S P E E D W A Y

9d

O F F I C I A L   P R O G R A M M E

Meetings promoted by Wembley Stadium Limited, Chairman and Managing Director, Sir Arthur J. Elvin, MBE
PROGRAMME OF THE 15th MEETING (22nd Season) **Thursday, August 30th, 1956, at 7.45 p.m.**
Meetings held under Speedway Regulations of the Speedway Control Board.   Permit No. S.P. 63.

Crutcher Qualifies for World Final
And Waterman may be There, Too !

pen and ink illustrations and in the text Hart not only outlined the history of the sport but also followed an imaginary Division Two rider throughout a typical week at the height of the season. The glamour, colour and heartache of speedway were captured in a publication which had a huge influence on the tastes of young boys. Hart himself did not enjoy any of the fabulous wealth he wrote about. Recalling the article many years later, he said he believed his fee had been 25s.

THERE IN 1956 – *Ray Cresp*

English speedway in the mid-1950s, despite the shrinking number of tracks, was still a magnet for overseas riders. The young hopefuls from Australia, New Zealand and South Africa who had traditionally flocked to the UK were increasingly being joined by riders from Scandinavia, with the difference being that, whether they succeeded or failed, riders from Down Under were in it for the long haul, lacking the Scandinavians' ability to get a ferry home.

After the closure of his first club, Wembley, Australian Ray Cresp rode for several British sides including Ipswich Witches. Six decades later, Ray cannot recall why the picture appears to have been taken in a railway goods yard!

One Australian prospect who found early success was Victorian Ray Cresp. After a brief period riding mainly in second halves he was catapulted to the ultimate league club, Wembley Lions, for a spell that was to prove brief but enjoyable. Cresp, a former middleweight boxer who did not ride a speedway machine until in his mid-twenties, started riding in Melbourne in 1954, using a bike he had bought from Harringay star and fellow Victorian Jack Biggs.

> I rode this bike through both the Australian 1954/55 and 1955/56 seasons. Jack had returned to Australia at the end of the English 1955 season during which, after the closure of Harringay, he had ridden for Poole.
>
> Jack saw me ride and suggested I go to England. The main problem was that with the downturn for speedway there, and tracks closing, there was no chance of me getting a fare over to the UK paid by a promoter. Jack said that he would be able to get me second-half rides at several tracks, so I took the chance and travelled to England as a freelance, arriving in time for the start of the 1956 season.
>
> I was more fortunate perhaps than many of the other riders coming to the UK [who] were without contacts. Jack Biggs showed me how to tune my bike and generally looked after me. I would not have made it without his help.

Jack Biggs was as good as his word in helping Ray find second-half rides. On Monday 30 April 1956 at Poole Stadium, the local Pirates beat Birmingham Brummies 54–30 in a league match, with Biggs and Jim Squibb each scoring 11 points for the home side.

Ray was one of the UK-based riders always prepared to ride in Europe. This shot in Amsterdam shows him keeping a particularly close eye on Olle Nygren's next move.

After the interval, the Cresp career took some of its first steps, as Ray earned his earliest English points money with a second place and a third in two of the evening's scratch races.

Further second-half appearances at Wimborne Road and elsewhere were followed by rides at Eastbourne, at the Arlington track owned and developed by pre-war rider Charlie Dugard, buried away in the Sussex countryside miles from the seaside resort from which it took its name.

Ray subsequently won the 1957 Sussex Championship, a prized individual honour dating back to the early 1930s, which had previously been won by veteran leg-trailer George Newton of New Cross and Birmingham's Phil Hart.

The Eastbourne booking which really mattered for Ray came a year earlier, and was an appearance for the Eagles team in the Southern Area League.

That was my big break in speedway. I had an exceptionally good meeting and Wembley signed me to a full contract on the back of this showing.

Ray's final British track was Long Eaton, from where he retired as a rider after the 1966 season. The riders in the background are Edinburgh Monarchs' Jimmy Tannock and Dud McKean.

Ray established a place in a Wembley team still full of big names. The points he scored were nevertheless welcome in a Lions side which had lost the twice World Champion Freddie Williams to retirement earlier in the season.

When Wembley scored a convincing 54–30 Division One victory over Belle Vue at the Empire Stadium in August 1956, Ray's 10 points made him second highest scorer in the side. Ray featured in Wembley's final home league match of the Sir Arthur Elvin era, against Norwich Stars on 30 August 1956, scoring 4 points and 2 bonus points in Wembley's narrow 43–41 victory.

In the winter of 1956/57 Ray raced in South Africa in a touring team put together by his team-mate Trevor Redmond and believes he heard the news of Wembley's withdrawal from the National League while still in the Union.

> It was certainly a shock to hear that Wembley was not opening for 1957. It was still a successful team, as we had finished runners-up to Wimbledon in the previous season.
>
> It was a blow for the sport in Britain and for me personally it was a great disappointment. I can't say enough good things about Wembley. They had a complete workshop and transport for all bikes to away meetings. I would class my time there as the highlight of my career.

Speedway moved on, despite the more pessimistic claiming that the death of Wembley would be the end of the sport. A single National League was formed from the survivors of the two divisions that had operated in 1956. Ray rode for Oxford in 1957, for Ipswich in 1958, moving with the Ipswich team to Poole for 1959, returning to Ipswich for 1960 and 1961.

Although he quit the sport temporarily to take up car racing in the early 1960s, he was persuaded to return to ride for Trevor Redmond's St Austell team in the Provincial League in 1963, although the Speedway Control Board was at first dubious about allowing a rider of Cresp's class and a fairly recent World Finalist to drop down a level.

That class was evident in 1964 when Ray rode successfully for the reopened West Ham in the National League, and when the National League and British League merged for 1965 he had two seasons at Long Eaton, top scoring for a struggling and injury-hit team. He stayed on as secretary of the Speedway Riders' Association before finally leaving for Australia with his wife Marion. His final comment on his career:

> I enjoyed my time in speedway and would love to have it over again.

CHAPTER TWELVE

1957

The survivors' tale

A cruel wind blew through speedway in early February 1957, with the iciest blasts coming from the Southern Hemisphere. Two deaths which occurred under the Southern Cross within the space of just a couple of days had a disruptive – and potentially fatal – effect on the sport at a time when it badly needed a prolonged period of stability.

The most stunning blow for the image of speedway was dealt by the death at sea of Wembley Stadium managing director Sir Arthur Elvin aboard a cruise liner bound for South Africa.

The second bolt from the blue was the death, following a track crash in Johannesburg, of Birmingham star Alan Hunt, who was leading a British touring side in the Union.

Elvin, in his late fifties, was a desperately sick man seeking a winter respite from illness in a kinder climate. Hunt was in his early thirties, at the height of his fame and popularity. Both deaths were tragedies inflicting grief not only of a personal nature, but also affecting speedway in general and its still substantial fan base. Elvin was not only a shrewd and successful businessman but also a genuine fan and a powerful champion of speedway. The story of how the young man from Norwich, who left school at fourteen, came to be the supremo of what was effectively England's national stadium reads like something from a self-help manual.

Wembley was built for the British Empire Exhibition of 1924, although it hosted the FA Cup final a year earlier. When the exhibition ended, the stadium appeared largely redundant, in an era when international football matches were few and far between and pop concerts were unknown.

Elvin, who during the exhibition had acquired the franchise to sell cigarettes from kiosks on site, now proved the unlikely saviour of the enterprise, as he brokered a complex deal under which he became the managing director of the company which now owned the whole stadium. Wembley became a viable sporting and business proposition not because of football, for which it was to become known worldwide, but because of the assured income generated by greyhound racing and speedway.

A sight never to be seen again after the mid-1950s – a Wembley Lions–Harringay Racers North London derby. Harringay's Lloyd Goffe is on the inside of Wembley's Freddie Williams, with Danny Dunton of the Racers on the outside.

The iconic sporting venue which for nearly three decades was virtually Elvin's personal fiefdom, where it was said even the track staff's rakes had to stand to attention. This view of the old Wembley was taken from the pits during a 1950s Test match, with more than 50,000 spectators in attendance.

When Elvin was planning the introduction of speedway to Wembley in 1929, he needed a manager with knowledge of the sport. Motorcycle enthusiast Lionel Wills, a wealthy scion of the Bristol-based tobacco family, had met Johnnie Hoskins during a visit to Australia, and he recommended the New Zealander to Elvin. The combination of a businessman and stickler for high standards, and the flamboyant showman, made a success of speedway at Wembley, after a faltering start. The Lions team they created caught the imagination of tens of thousands of people. The tussles for supremacy

After the closure of Wembley for league racing, the final pride of Lions dispersed. Tommy Price, a Wembley rider for his entire career, apart from 1930s loan spells elsewhere, retired.

throughout the 1930s between Wembley Lions and northern counterparts Belle Vue Aces are the very stuff of speedway legend.

After the departure of Hoskins to run his own show at West Ham, Elvin continued to insist on consistent on-track success for the Lions. However, in the mid-1950s, crowds had dwindled even at Wembley and the team was in a period of rebuilding as the stars of the immediate post-war years retired or became less effective as advancing years took their toll.

The prevailing view in speedway nevertheless was that the sport had a future at Wembley as long as Elvin remained at the helm. As an apparently still vigorous man in his mid-fifties, there was no suggestion that he was about to retire or be ousted by his fellow directors, despite an apparent dislike for speedway in some quarters of the boardroom.

The news from the South Atlantic changed everything. The Wembley directors took the opportunity to opt out of league speedway, with an announcement in March 1957 that the Lions would not compete in Division One in the forthcoming season, although the stadium would still continue to be available for the World Final. What might have happened in 1957 had Elvin lived and the Lions survived is still a matter for conjecture. The pressure for one big league might nevertheless have become irresistible.

It is hard to imagine that Coventry promoter Charles Ochiltree had any form of second sight when, in his final programme notes for 1956, he confidently predicted that there *would* be one big league in 1957. Wembley had always operated somewhat as a law unto itself in speedway terms and Ochiltree's end of season report was highly critical of the Lions management for being the only track to refuse to compete in the inter-division tournament staged in 1956 to pad out a fixture list sadly depleted by track closures.

Writing more than half a century later, in the knowledge that speedway not only survived the closure of Wembley as a league team but went on to enjoy another golden age in the late 1960s and 1970s, it would be easy to scoff at the predictions of doom that followed the announcement of Wembley's withdrawal.

For some commentators Wembley's withdrawal from league racing was not just the end of an era but spelled the end for speedway as a whole. The specialist speedway media, from its origins in the early days of the sport, had an identifiable London bias. One of the arguments used against automatic promotion and relegation was the claim that the provincial tracks that were allowed to compete in Division One in the 1940s and early '50s were unattractive visitors to the homes of the London 'big five'.

Speedway's changing face saw Test matches between England and Poland. The Eastern European nation was represented at Birmingham by, left to right, Florian Kapala, Mieczyslaw Polukard (team manager), Edward Kupczynski, Eugeniusz Nazimek, Tadeusz Teodorowicz and Wlodz Szwendrowski. Teodorowicz later defected and was killed racing in England.

Wembley was not lost to speedway altogether. World Finals and other major events took place for another three decades, and there was a brief 1970s league revival, which proved incompatible with modern football demands. New Zealander Barry Briggs, twenty-three years old in 1957, lifted the 1957 title, defeating the Norwich duo of Fundin and Lawson.

The closure of three of the London Division One tracks in the space of three consecutive years – New Cross in 1953, Harringay at the end of 1954 and West Ham a year later – was a bitter enough blow for many commentators to bear. The disappearance of Wembley was for them the final straw. Many years later, one of the most influential of speedway journalists was still driven to write:

> A league with Wembley mattered. The league, when it became without Wembley, didn't matter. It slumped down, down, down after the famous Lions had disbanded.

It didn't, actually. Speedway, as ever, pulled itself together manfully as the opening date for the 1957 season approached. The worst blow to the sport might well have been

Following Wembley's demise the rest of the decade saw plenty of questions being asked of the sport. Two of speedway's deepest thinkers, Barry Briggs (left) and Ray Cresp, take time to consider the issues. Briggs was arguably the rider best known to the media while Cresp served as a respected secretary of the Speedway Riders' Association.

not the loss of Wembley as *the* prestige venue and the league club that impressed even a cynical Fleet Street, but as an indirect funder of a significant part of the rest of the Division One structure.

Wembley stalwart and twice World Champion Freddie Williams has a particular viewpoint on what may well have been Wembley's greatest area of influence in the early to mid-1950s. The Wembley riders in that final Empire Stadium summer of 1956 could not ignore the warning signs of thinning crowds at the Empire Stadium, and decline in enthusiasm. When Elvin died unexpectedly, the withdrawal of Wembley from league racing was a disappointment but not, he admits, a real shock. As he explained:

> Although Wembley had enjoyed big crowds over the years, presenting speedway in such a huge stadium meant a lot of expense, and for Elvin, everything had to be perfect.

A great admirer of Elvin, Freddie believes that the majority of people in the mid-1950s, even those on the inside of speedway, were unaware of the role the Wembley chairman played in keeping the sport alive.

> Elvin really loved his speedway. People made a great thing out of Wembley's importance from a public relations point of view, believing that if the Lions continued to be part of speedway, the sport would still have status.
>
> What was not generally realised was that Elvin and Wembley were indirectly financially subsidising the other surviving Division One tracks, particularly in London.

When Wembley visited New Cross, Elvin took ten per cent of the gate. When New Cross rode at Wembley they also had ten per cent of the takings. But with Wembley's crowds being so big, the value of ten per cent at the Empire Stadium was much higher than at New Cross.

He realised that if he did not help other tracks in this way, the whole business would collapse.

There has been much discussion over the years about what might have happened had Elvin not died at the comparatively young age of fifty-seven. Williams has a realistic view:

We should never forget that despite his love for speedway, Elvin was first and foremost a businessman. Whether he could have convinced the Wembley directors to continue financing a league team indefinitely is something we will never know. Whether [his] head would eventually have overruled his heart is again something we can only guess at.

The remaining promoters in 1957 absorbed the loss not only of Wembley, but also the closure of two further Division One tracks, Poole and Bradford. The single league confidently predicted by Charles Ochiltree came into being with the four Division One survivors joining forces with the seven Division Two tracks to form a viable eleven-member National League.

Promoter Les Marshall's efforts to keep the sport running at Perry Barr were further weakened by the death of Alan Hunt. The Aston-born rider was hugely popular in his home city and Birmingham's struggles after his death had echoes of the situation at New Cross a few years before, where enthusiasm had never been quite the same after the loss of form and departure of another idol, Ron Johnson.

Swindon, Division Two champions in 1956, surprised the speedway world by winning the merged National League at the first attempt, interrupting the winning streak of Wimbledon. Back row, left to right: Bob Roger, Ian Williams, Bob Jones (team manager), Neil Street and Ernie Lessiter. Front row: Ken Middleditch, George White and Mike Broadbank.

There was only one holder of the match race championship in 1957, Peter Craven, seen on the centre green at his home track, Belle Vue, with the coveted golden helmet.

A sure sign of success in speedway is a settled team and the Swindon riders pictured celebrating their championship success with promoter Bert Hearse (left), mechanics, track staff and ecstatic fans are the same septet that rode through most of the season. Nobody in this Blunsdon picture believed speedway was dying in 1957!

To make matters even worse, Marshall's team-building plans for 1957 were rocked by the announcement of the suspension of the best part of his team, who were ruled by the Control Board to have raced illegally in South Africa during the English winter tour.

The troubles in South Africa essentially arose out of a dispute between rival promoters. The suspensions were eventually lifted but it was too late to save the Brummies. The death of league speedway at what was effectively the national stadium and in the nation's second city were hammer blows.

The sport, again displaying that feline propensity for jumping straight into a new life out of what had appeared to be potential oblivion, yet again found a solution to its problems.

Although Bradford had quit Division One at the end of the previous campaign, the track had been granted a 1957 licence for open meetings. When the Brummies closed down, the Yorkshire track was able to step into the breach. The pundits stepped back from the predictions of imminent doom and the 1957 season continued. For the first time for many years there were no Test matches in England of any kind (they would resume in 1958) and although the Lions were roaring no longer there was at least the reassurance of a World Championship final night at Wembley, with a first victory for Barry Briggs, with rivals Ove Fundin and Peter Craven occupying the other spots on the victory podium.

The huge surprise was the success of Swindon in winning the new, one-division, National League, with Belle Vue in second place and Wimbledon down in a (by now) unaccustomed third spot.

Swindon, Division Two champions the previous year, had generally only been in the running for the title of the sport's most unfashionable team. The Robins however, were truly a *team*, and this was the major contributing factor to their success. Swindon benefited from the fact that Poole had dropped out of speedway for a year and they were able to track a rider of the ability of Ken Middleditch, while men like George White, Mike Broadbank and Bob Roger, comparative failures elsewhere, blossomed at Blunsdon under the wing of former skipper, now team manager, Bob Jones, while Ian Williams was given every opportunity to develop without undue pressure.

The crucial factor that transformed the team into champions was the signing of Australian Neil Street, a former Exeter rider, who returned from Down Under to complete the Blunsdon jigsaw. The sheer team power of Swindon, particularly at Blunsdon, was demonstrated when the Robins beat Birmingham 77–19 in the National League in June, with all six of the home riders, except the reserve, returning double-figure scores.

In the Southern Area League, now the second tier of speedway in England, the Southern Rovers found a home at Rayleigh and celebrated by winning the championship, with three-times victors Rye House finding themselves at the opposite end of the table.

At the end of the 1957 season, as all concerned with speedway caught their collective breath, it must have been obvious to everyone that despite the disasters of mid-decade, the sport would live on.

THE GOLDEN AGE OF SPEEDWAY

The rapid expansion in the late 1940s had been achieved on the tail of a massive public hunger for entertainment of any kind. It was said of the era that if a couple of men began to play marbles in the street, a crowd would gather. It was a public attitude that could not last. For some years, attendances at most (if not all) tracks were large enough to withstand the strain of the punitive entertainment tax. The immediate post-war surge of support for virtually any form of sport or entertainment was a by-product of the immense public relief at the end of the uncertainty, suffering and deprivation experienced during the wartime years and a reluctance to immediately return to pre-war levels of domesticity. When, as was inevitable, the public mood began to settle down, and returning servicemen and their wives starting to raise families – the baby boomer generation – there was both less cash to spend and less inclination to spend what was available outside the increasingly important home environment.

The 1950s saw a great increase in expectations of a more comfortable home among speedway's core audience, the working classes. It also brought television. It is difficult now, in an age of so much electronic entertainment, to describe the immense novelty of the cramped, black and white, single (and later double) channel TV of the era. Millions watched virtually every hour of the restricted programming, including many who were no longer prepared to swap their armchairs for a place on the terrace of their local speedway track.

The eleven tracks that raced the crucial 1957 season and the ten that surfaced again in 1958 gave the sport a relatively stable platform on which to base its eventual comeback. They were the tracks that had learnt to cut their coats according to the available cloth. The high operating costs of the London stadia and the often unrealistic rent rises demanded by the stadium owners, at a time when greyhound racing was still popular and highly profitable, undoubtedly helped to bring about the virtual decimation of speedway in the capital city in the mid-1950s.

It is a tribute to the persistence of Ronnie Greene at Wimbledon that the sport survived at the South London track as long as it did, no doubt helped by a certain number of spectators from the closed venues who were prepared to make the trek from one side of London to another to get their speedway fix.

Outside of London, it was the well-organised, well-managed and still relatively well-supported clubs such as Coventry, Swindon, Norwich and Southampton who formed the absolute hardcore of the sport and allowed it to consolidate and even plan for the future. Belle Vue, in the form in which it existed for many years, was a special case. Speedway at Hyde Road was an integral part of a much larger entertainment complex, with a zoo, funfair, ballrooms and bars within the grounds. Speedway matches and stock car meetings started early and finished on the dot, to allow the crowds to flock from the stands and terraces into the other constituent parts of the complex and spend more money. The complex eventually became another victim of changing leisure tastes. As the zoo and other facilities disappeared, the speedway became isolated. The health and safety scare resulting from the disastrous fire at Bradford City was perhaps the immediate cause of why the largely wooden speedway stadium became unsustainable, but it would have needed large-scale modernisation in any case.

Looking back on a departed golden era? Some of speedway's greatest talent, gathered together at Wembley on a World Final night, are actually watching the first heat with expressions of mixed emotions, from pleasure in taking part to high tension. Left to right are Arthur Forrest, Alan Hunt, Freddie Williams, Aub Lawson, Ronnie Moore, Jack Young, Geoff Mardon, Split Waterman and Ove Fundin.

Throughout the 1950s people from all over the north and the Midlands travelled by coach or train to the Belle Vue complex for a day out, often as visitors to a brass band or other festival. A significant number of these people stayed for the early evening speedway meeting, ensuring that crowds for the Aces matches remained generally healthy.

Not all of those tracks which survived the mid-1950s speedway decline were quite as prosperous as those mentioned beforehand. Crowds were steadily dwindling at Leicester and were rocky at Oxford, Rayleigh and Ipswich, with the latter two tracks experiencing a yo-yo existence.

Despite Bradford's availability to take over Birmingham's fixtures midway through 1957, the Odsal side dropped out again at the end of the campaign. Fortunately, Poole returned after just a year's absence – Rayleigh actually raced some of their later 1957 fixtures at Wimborne Road – and the second post-Wembley season of 1958 was assured of viability.

Significantly, both in 1957 and later in the decade, men – often former riders – were willing to invest in short seasons of open racing at tracks such as Exeter, Liverpool and Motherwell, particularly after the Conservative government abolished entertainment tax completely in 1957. Eventually, the groundwork was put in place for the subsequent success of the Provincial League.

Could speedway's administrators and promoters have done more to arrest the sport's decline in the 1950s? The question of whether or not the men who laid down the strategies and tactics for speedway, and controlled the purse strings, failed the riders and supporters, and the question of whether or not greater investment could and should have been made in terms of facilities, can trigger a passionate debate even today, and among the best of speedway friends.

Ove Fundin is proud of not only his own achievements but also those of his native country. The sport in Sweden is thriving today largely, he believes, because of the vision of its promoters in the 1950s. He explained:

> The clubs in Sweden made sure that they owned the stadium where they raced. It meant that the tracks could not be sold under the clubs for development.
>
> Many of the British promoters in the 1940s and 1950s were only in the sport to make their own money. When so many of the stadiums were sold for building projects, they had nowhere else to go, especially with noise and other regulations getting stricter. I do believe that if the sport in the UK had been more independent and owned its own tracks, it would have been in a much stronger position today.

Ove Fundin's great rival, Barry Briggs, is also on record as criticising the lack of investment by British speedway promoters in the fat years. In his 2010 book *Wembley and Beyond* Briggs said:

> When speedway was at its best with enormous crowds and plenty of money coming through the turnstiles, nothing was put back into tracks, especially the safety fences.

Ove's friend Reg Fearman takes a different position, describing the debate as a conversion he and Ove have often had over the years.

> Ove has always criticised the British speedway promoters for not building their own stadia. The problem has always been finding the land in a small country which even in the 1950s had a population of 50 million plus and today has 60 million. That is not to mention the funding for the purchase and the development of a track and spectator facilities.
>
> In Britain speedway has largely survived through the efforts of the individual entrepreneur. For decades this was usually a former rider, going back as far as the 1930s and the efforts of Bluey Wilkinson at Sheffield and Max Groskreutz at Norwich, right up to myself, Danny Dunton and many others.
>
> The big difference is that Sweden is almost twice the size of Britain with a population of some 8 million people. No speedways there run with an individual promoter, they are all organised through motor clubs, as in Germany and other countries.
>
> Sweden has plenty of space to build tracks, with little fear of rejection from the powers that be. So with our different points of view, the conversations and discussions between Ove and myself will go on.
>
> Over the years we have built stadia. Charlie Dugard and his family at Eastbourne have showed great foresight in buying and developing Arlington and I was involved in a new stadium at Reading, while the late 1960s saw a great deal of development at Coventry.

Maximum concentration, maximum determination. Ove Fundin was one of the most controversial, as well as one of the most successful, riders of all time. His presence in the programme brought the crowds through the turnstiles.

THERE IN 1957 – *Ove Fundin*

Ove Fundin has no patience with the once widespread belief among some speedway commentators that the sport effectively died with the 1957 closure of Wembley as a league team. Fundin, whose views on speedway are as strong as the competitive spirit which fired him to five World Championships, had already won his first title, in 1956, and was by the start of the 1957 season an established member of the Norwich team, which he was to serve until The Firs Stadium was sold for housing development and closed at the end of the 1964 season.

Although he obviously accepts that the sport in Britain had declined from its high point in the late 1940s, with fewer tracks and smaller crowds, Ove still regards the period from his British debut in a match for a Swedish touring team at Rayleigh in 1953 right through to the end of the decade as both a golden period for his personal career and a time when crowds at the UK's surviving tracks saw speedway of the highest class.

My main racing career lasted until 1970 and even since my retirement I have been closely involved in speedway racing all over the world. Looking back, I think the supporters and the riders enjoyed their speedway in those years even more than in other eras.

Although a lot of tracks had closed, the crowds were certainly there in the mid- to late 1950s at the places that remained open. Norwich, where I rode from 1954 right up until it closed, averaged between 8,000 and 9,000.

Maximum respect. Ove, world champion again in 1960 and match race champion, receives the congratulations of another long-serving Norwich Star, Aub Lawson, who retired after that season.

The newspapers were still full of reports of meetings and other speedway stories, and the major competitions, like the World Championship, were sponsored by papers like the *Sunday Pictorial* and the *Sunday Mirror*, at a time when sponsorship of any kind was rare in sport.

We still had royalty and other important people attending meetings and presenting prizes, both in the UK and in Sweden. I met the King of Sweden on more than one occasion and, in the UK, Prince Philip and Prince Rainier of Monaco, who was a great fan of speedway.

The smallest attendance I can remember at Wembley for a World Final was 64,000 people. At Norwich on one occasion they sold 6,000 tickets for a Wembley final, with people travelling to London not only by coach but also by special trains.

It was a good time to be a speedway rider. I played golf with some of the Norwich City footballers, who were still on a fixed wage and earning quite a lot less in the summer than in the season. They were quite envious of me because football was and still is the top sport; I could make as much in one night at speedway as they earned for a week – and I was riding virtually seven days a week in England, at home in Sweden or elsewhere.

Sometimes in that period, including spending a winter in Australia, I was riding 150 meetings a year, with most of the travelling done by car.

Today I hear a lot of stories about how much riders are demanding from the sport. In the 1950s nearly all riders were earning just their start and points money and travelling expenses. I was never paid a penny above that, although Norwich provided me with a bike and paid for my journeys between Sweden and England, something the speedway authorities insisted upon in those days.

Major Bill Fearnley, secretary of the Speedway Board of Control, tosses the coin for gate position at Norwich as Ove Fundin prepares to (successfully) defend his match race title against Leicester Hunters' Scottish star Ken McKinlay. The year is 1962, when Fundin beat off all challenges to his individual dominance.

Most of the riders at the time, and right throughout speedway's most popular years, had a job or a business. I started my business in 1959.

What was special about Norwich? I don't think there was anything particularly special to bring about the track's success. People around there certainly liked speedway. Although Norwich is a fairly big city there was not a lot going on apart from football and speedway.

The football team played on a Saturday afternoon and we rode at The Firs on a Saturday evening. I don't think many people went first to the football and then to the speedway. It was a different crowd, with many speedway supporters coming in from the country areas around the city.

I know this was the case with many of my strongest personal fans, many of whom still write to me today. There was very much a family spirit at Norwich, and I think at most of the other tracks and that is something which still exists in speedway today.

From 1954 to the end of 1964 I rode only for Norwich in England and the majority of the other riders stayed with one team. It helped to create a strong team spirit and a bond with the supporters. It created local heroes.

I go back to Norwich quite often and I was proud to be made a Freeman of the City – an honour I share with Admiral Lord Nelson. I am the only sportsman to date to receive the honour.

Was it a dark time for speedway? I saw it as the best time of my life for sure. I am sure I would not have enjoyed speedway so much as it is at the present time.

Not many people rode for the money. We rode for the glory. To win was the most important thing, not only for yourself but for your team and for your country.

I get a bid mad when people claim that winning the World Championship in the days of a one-off World Final was easier than competing on the Grand Prix circuit. The Grand Prix idea is a good one in itself, but people could not be more wrong when they say the old system was easier. You had to take part in several qualifying rounds to get through to the final. Anything could go wrong during those qualifiers and again on the night. It was a real test of men and machines and who could keep their nerve on a big occasion at a packed Wembley.

Appendix

THE POST-WAR HONOURS LIST – 1946 TO 1957

British Riders Championship
1946: Tommy Price
1947: Jack Parker
1948: Vic Duggan

British Match Race C/ship
1946: Bill Kitchen, Jack Parker
1947: J. Parker, Vic Duggan, J. Parker
1948: J. Parker
1949: J. Parker
1950: J. Parker, Aub Lawson
1951: A. Lawson, J. Parker, Split Waterman
1952: S. Waterman, Jack Young
1953: J. Young, Ronnie Moore
1954: R. Moore, Arthur Forrest, R. Moore
1955: R. Moore, J. Young
1956: R. Moore, Brian Crutcher, Peter Craven
1957: P. Craven

The World Championship
1949: Tommy Price
1950: Fred Williams
1951: Jack Young
1952: Jack Young
1953: Fred Williams
1954: Ronnie Moore
1955: Peter Craven
1956: Ove Fundin
1957: Barry Briggs

National Trophy
1946: Belle Vue	1952: Harringay
1947: Belle Vue	1953: Wimbledon
1948: Wembley	1954: Wembley
1949: Belle Vue	1955: Norwich
1950: Wimbledon	1956: Wimbledon
1951: Wimbledon	1957: Not raced

LEAGUE RACING

National League
1946: Wembley

Division One
1947: Wembley
1948: New Cross
1949: Wembley

Northern League
1946: Middlesbrough

Division Two
1947: Middlesbrough
1948: Bristol
1949: Bristol

Division Three
1947: Eastbourne
1948: Exeter
1949: Hanley
1950: Oxford
1951: Poole

Division One
1950: Wembley
1951: Wembley
1952: Wembley
1953: Wembley
1954: Wimbledon
1955: Wimbledon
1956: Wimbledon

Coronation Cup

National League
1957: Swindon

Division Two
1950: Norwich
1951: Norwich
1952: Poole
1953: Coventry
1954: Bristol
1955: Poole
1956: Swindon

1953: Harringay

Southern League
1952: Rayleigh
1953: Exeter

Southern Area League
1954: Rye House
1955: Rye House
1956: Rye House
1957: Rayleigh Rovers

Official Test Matches raced in England
1947: England 2 Australia 1
1948: England 4 Australia 1
1949: England 2 Australia 3
1950: England 3 Australia 2
1951: England 1 Australia 4
1952: England 1 Australia 4
1953: England 2 Australia 1

1954: England 3 Australasia 0
1955: England 4 Australasia 2
1956: England 3 Australasia 0
1957: No series

1956: England 1 Sweden 2
1957: Not raced

Printed in Great Britain
by Amazon